Leaves Of Maple

An Illinois State University Professor's Memoirs Of Seven Summers Teaching In Canadian Universities, 1972-1978

G. Louis Heath, Ph.D

Leaves Of Maple

An Illinois State University Professor's Memoirs Of Seven Summers Teaching In Canadian Universities, 1972-1978

By

G. Louis Heath, Ph.D.

1stBooks - rev. 1/2/01

For my students at Illinois State University, especially Larry Burdette, Holly Fuller, Carey Anderson, Chris Kapraun, Pam Blankenship, Barb Weeks, Colleen Quigley, Sandy Silvis, Kathy Geary, Marsha Brown, Rhetta Smith, Patti Viteele, Brenda Boyd, Kris Koppen, Tyrone Bentley, Debbie Weber, Giacomina St. Angel, Ronald Zemke, Linda Scott, Charles Brooks, Bernadette Daily, Roger Reiner, Marcia McClendon, Patti Mahoney, Sheri Vopalensky, Fonda Baron, Sue Koch, Luanne Daucanski, Mary Licari, Laurie Myhre, Michele Davis, Emmanuel Tepi, José Ignacio Regalado, Tammy Simonek, Rosemary Yocum, Jean English, Robert Hull, Kevin Randall, and Patricia Joseph.

Table Of Contents

Chapter 1

McGill University, 1972

Canada. Images of hockey, the Maple-Leaf Flag, Mounties, lakes filled with trout, majestic mountains off which one skied, and a vast prairie of farms that help feed the world. I had a few vague impressions that amounted to knowing almost nothing. That was the state of my knowledge prior to teaching, researching, and writing seven consecutive summers, coast to coast, at Canadian universities.

I had met a few Canadians before coming to Canada, as a student during the sixties at the Berkeley campus of the University of California. They didn't seem any different from the Americans except they poured a lot of sugar into their coffee and they had the stinky habit of dousing their French fries with vinegar. After lunch with the Canadians, I'd walk about campus inside a vinegary vapor all day. And I even had to tell one badly informed Canadian physics Ph.D. student that the French fries weren't called "chips," that that term referred to "dried cow dung."

I also recall the Berkeley Canadians saying "eh?" whenever they became excited or reached the end of a sentence. A group of Ethiopian students at International House, where I lived, devoted a lot of time to mimicking this "eh?," exploding into uproarious laughter at their exaggerated renditions.

This gives you the flavor of my early knowledge of Canada. Impressionistic, sketchy, and based on Hollywood stereotypes and meeting a handful of Canadians in California.

In the fall of 1971, I thumbed through a textbook on Canadian geography that one of my students at Illinois State University had left on his tablet-arm chair. As I perused the thick volume, I noted that the chapters were written by Canadian professors whose names were followed by their university affiliations.

1

I immediately remembered what a Canadian economics Ph.D. student, Mel Fuss, had told me at Berkeley—that Canadian universities often hired American professors to teach summer sessions. Mel regarded this as healthy, invigorating intellectual exchange, an exchange that he at the time, spring, 1969, was about to be party to as he prepared to leave for a four-year contract at Harvard University. (Mel: "John Kenneth Galbraith is not really an economist, not a **real** economist. Some of the real economists at Harvard wonder what he's doing in the field. He's more a popular writer than anything else.")

As I studied that geography book, I thought that teaching at one of the Canadian universities might prove interesting. I copied the names of three universities, including McGill, that I had heard of, and sent out letters the next day inquiring about the prospects for summer teaching. That was in November, 1971.

Long after I had forgotten those letters, in March, 1972, Dr. Roger Magnuson, Chairman of the History, Philosophy, and Sociology of Education Department in McGill University's Faculty of Education, phoned and offered me a summer job. I accepted. A week later, a contract arrived in the mail that read:

March 17, 1972

Dr. G. Louis Heath
College of Education
Illinois State University
Normal, Illinois 61761

Dear Dr. Heath:

The following are the terms of appointment of Dr. G. Louis Heath to the teaching staff of the Summer Session of McGill University, agreed upon by the undersigned.

COURSE: 413-627C PHILOSOPHICAL ANALYSIS AND THE PROBLEMS OF EDUCATION

2

DURATION: July 4 – August 11
REMUNERATION: $1,900
HOURS PER DAY: 8 a.m. – 10 a.m.

_____

Signature of Instructor

(signed)

_____

Gordon W. E. McElroy
Director, Summer Session
McGill University

Date: March 22, 1972

Travel expenses equivalent to round trip, air fare, economy rates.

I signed this contract on March 22nd and mailed it back to McGill University.

I left Illinois in early June, entering Canada by way of New York State. I first went to Toronto, staying three weeks at Tartu College, a high-rise, largely student residence on Bloor Street, from where I took in the fun and sights of the city.

In Toronto I met a lot of interesting people, ate lunch at an Eaton's department store cafeteria, drank my first Molson's beer, took a ferry ride to nearby islands in Lake Ontario, and attended an international festival where I bobbed from one ethnic enclave to another, tasting a wide range of delicious foods and watching more folk dances than I care to remember. Also, importantly for my writing, I became acquainted with the superb fiction of

3

author Hugh Garner, whose Depression-era novel **Cabbagetown** thoroughly engrossed and impressed me and whose short stories I have come to regard as among the best the English language has to offer.

I also read a good many articles and books about Québec while in Toronto, so that I would be more informed about the province when I arrived in Montreal.

I experienced difficulty leaving Montreal on the national holiday, Dominion Day, a Monday, the day before my class at McGill University was to begin. My car would not start and I needed a running push from two, helpful, young men. It was exhilarating to get under way, but I knew the problem was far from over. My car needed a major overhaul. Through previous, tortured experience, I knew that, should I pull over, I would doubtless need another push. Nevertheless, I pulled the boner I was hoping to avoid when I stopped for gas at a Shell "service centre" on Highway 401. Damn if I didn't unthinkingly switch the ignition off.

The two attendants who serviced my car, one of them a quick-to-smile University of Toronto student, gave me another running push. Huffing and straining at full stride, they found themselves in danger of joining the traffic north on 401 when, near where the approach lane met the highway, my engine finally kicked over, drawing me away from their arms stretched forward in pushing positions. Evidently seeing humor in their positions at the apron of the highway -- fellows about to run north on 401! -- they threw back their heads and laughed, waving brusquely at me in gestures that said jocularly, "Good riddance!" Feeling exceedingly grateful to be under way again, I glanced over my shoulder and beamed my best Yankee smile of appreciation.

I knew I had to find a place to live, at least for one night, in sprawling, unfamiliar Montreal, without cutting the ignition. I didn't advance my cause one bit by immediately becoming quite lost in the city's maze of freeways, ending up in a suburb asking for directions. Finally, I managed to get into the city proper where I cruised about, crossing and re-crossing Ste. Catherine, Dorchester, Décarie, Masoineuve and other main thoroughfares until I happened upon the university. I soon located the building on McTavish Street where I would work, the Faculty of Education, a modern, brick-and-glass split-level fitted onto the side of steep Mount Royal.

Fine so far, I thought. You're doing OK. Now find a place to stay and don't turn off your engine while you're at it.

I began to drive the streets on the city-side flank of Mount Royal. On the north side of campus, on Aylmer Street and on Park Street, I descried several ancient, mellow mansions with "Rooms For Rent" signs that looked like possibilities. However, when I took a look, I found the places too noisy, dirty, or just plain student-infested.

I persevered in driving up and down, to and fro, along what I began to think of as "The Hill," after a British film by the same name starring a sadistic infantry officer who trained raw recruits beyond their endurance on a mammoth, sand hill. I imagined that I and my car, "Old Illinois," were being put similarly to the test on another, much more challenging acclivity, Mount Royal. I was very impressed with the sheer steepness and breadth of the mountain, features I was to pit myself against on foot throughout the summer and into autumn.

I was soon driving Pine Avenue, a one-way thoroughfare that ran level along an engineering cut in the mountain. As I passed the Royal Victoria Hospital, a stolid, quarry-stone complex above me, I could see the brick-and-stone buildings of the compact McGill campus to my left, down the hill below. The salient architecture of the campus jutted above the maple trees, like impassive sentinels for that beguiling Anglophone bridgehead of intellectual endeavor.

Not far from campus, I saw a crackled, black-on-white sign on an old, three-story, brick building: "Pine Avenue House, 1280 Pine Ave. W., Rooms For Rent, Tel. 842-6556. VACANCY." The façade looked more appealing than anything I had seen till then, and I had to admit it was conveniently located, only three

5

blocks from the Faculty of Education. So, I pulled my car over and parked, and, of course, left the motor running.

A dumpy, sleepy-looking woman sat behind the registration desk, blabbing over the phone and smoking. Her cigarette gyrated in one corner of her mouth as she talked out of the other corner. The top of her squat body was garbed in a blue lamé, Western-style shirt that had patch pockets, each containing a pack of cigarettes, one soft, one hard. Her dishwater-brown hair was pulled back tautly and secured into a ponytail with a garish, blaze-orange barrette. This Pine Avenue House cowgirl acknowledged my presence with a slight nod, gave a stingy, wooden smile through her tobacco-stained teeth, and continued her eminently stupid gabfest.

I sat down on a sofa in the lobby and gazed out a window, studying the late afternoon sunlight filtering through a stand of birch trees across the street. The broken-toothed cowgirl talked on and on and I shifted my attention to a striped cat sleeping at the base of a soft-drink-dispensing machine. When I heard the phone receiver plunked back upon its cradle, I stood up and said I wanted to look at a room.

The woman gave me a little smirk I couldn't fathom and said she'd get her boss. She disappeared and soon returned with a lantern-jawed, sixtyish woman who was decidedly overdressed for the neighborhood. She wore a light blue, alpaca sweater over a green, silk blouse, a pair of expensively tailored, fawn, wool slacks and snakeskin shoes. Her bleary eyes were etched with tiny, red veins and she had her pet, eight-foot-long boa constrictor, "Pierre," cuddled affectionately about her neck. I didn't know what to make of her except that she looked interesting as hell.

"Hello, my name is Leila. Can I help you?" said the landlady in a contralto voice as her boa constrictor yawned.

"Yes, I hope so," I replied. "I need a room." The big snake closed its yap, completing its yawn. "I'm here to teach at McGill," I added. I threw in this information to point up my respectability, though I felt sure the only reference I needed was cash payment and a genuine affection for boa constrictors of French-Canadian descent.

"Let me show you what we have," smiled Leila, setting "Pierre" down on his scales and plucking a key off a hook on a large, plywood board. She led me out of the main lobby up steps covered with worn carpeting, fumigating the stairway with the scent of the patchouli she must've bathed in with that damn snake.

Leila stopped at a room at the end of the hall, unlocked the door, and showed me in. It was a good-sized, clean room, featuring a desk and lamp, a large closet, and close proximity to the hallway bathroom.

Next, Leila took me to another floor to a huge kitchen and pantry that hinted at a grander time of the stately, old building. Then to a broad verandah in the back that ran the length of the building on the second story. Leila called it a "sun deck." From it, I enjoyed a great, picture-postcard view of downtown Montreal and the St. Lawrence River beyond. I thought Montreal, at the time one, of the most beautiful cities imaginable. Subsequent, far-flung travel has firmed up that initial impression.

I told Leila I'd take the room and hustled outside to pull my car over onto a concrete parking area beside the building. I triumphantly extracted the key from the ignition. My car had made its way to a well-earned rest. It would sit there six weeks until three friendly Pine Avenue residents gave me one final push, one that would take me to the repair garage.

I rushed back in and paid Leila $75 cash, a month's rent, which was plenty enough in the days of the eight-cent, first-class postage stamp. "Pierre" seemed real happy that I was going to live near him, and I was equally pleased we weren't going to be roommates.

I got up early, 6:30, the next morning, Tuesday, July 4th and prepared to meet my eight o'clock class. (Monday, July 3rd, had been an employee holiday at McGill University and everywhere else in Canada in celebration of Dominion Day, July 1, the date of Canada's founding, which had fallen on the previous Sunday.) I wanted to inspire alertness, confidence, and interest in my students by appearing alert, confident, and interesting myself. To be that, I have to be up and about at least an hour before class and drink two or more cups of strong, black coffee. Accordingly, I proceeded to shower, have my coffee, read the paper, and go over my class notes. Last, I dressed in a royal blue blazer, navy blue slacks, and blue-and-gold tie. Then I bounded out of the building full of enthusiasm, literally craving to teach my first class.

I walked along Pine Avenue toward McGill in the brilliant sun that illumined the east face of Mount Royal, passing the modern, high-rise L'Horizon Apartments and enjoying the iridescent play of light on the dew covering nearby lawn and flowers. It would have been a great time to be outside rather than teaching. I could see warblers titupping through trees and shrubbery and the scent of several varieties of flowers registered pleasurably with me. I comforted myself with the thought that my class only ran from eight to ten and that I would soon be out in the beauty of Montreal.

I came to the intersection of Pine Avenue and McTavish Street where a tall, wrought-iron fence guards an imposing mansion housing a McGill University physics research institute. At this solid, granite building, I turned right and was soon at the Faculty of Education building.

I entered and made my way toward the seminar room assigned me on the second floor, my feet slipping on highly waxed floors. I stopped at a water fountain for a sip of water and to adjust my tie.

I entered my seminar room, fixing what I hoped was a confident, alert, interesting expression on my face. Before me sat ten graduate students—seven men, three women—around a glossy, walnut, conference table. The women smiled a little and the men tried to convey a powerful intelligence (or, was it simply power?). The ten, most of them in their twenties and thirties, were waiting, like students always do, for the professor (this one aged 27, soon to be 28) to make things happen.

"Good morning," I smiled. "I am Dr. Heath, and this is Education 413, Philosophical Analysis and the Problems of Education." I paused to see if anyone would be prompted to say he was in the wrong room. (No one was.) "I'm your basic, visiting professor from Illinois, hired to teach this one summer course," I continued by way of introduction. "I've been looking forward to teaching here. I hope to get to know each of you. Maybe we can stir up some educational excitement. Perhaps we can ruffle still waters with our brilliant, incisive, philosophical analyses."

"One thing I absolutely refuse to do is lecture 100% of the time at you and wait for you to ask questions. That format doesn't make for a good graduate seminar. You're too smart and advanced for that, so I'll be doing my best to get you involved. And please feel free to interrupt me at any time, especially if you disagree. I like dissidents."

"Now let me give you an opportunity to introduce yourselves." I pointed to the student nearest me. "We'll start with you."

The young, bearded man I indicated was René Fouchard, a University of Montreal master's degree candidate. He was taking my course, needed for his M.A., because it was not offered that summer on the French side of Mount Royal at his own university.

Seated beside René was an attractive, young woman in roll-necked, yellow sweater and white duck slacks. Her almond eyes projected a haunting softness beneath her luxuriant jet-black pageboy. She was Lucy Cohn, a Montreal elementary school teacher.

Sudi Ambardeckar, the only student wearing a suit and tie, was an immigrant, middle-aged Indian who taught high school math in a Montreal suburb. "The greed for money that the Canadians and Americans have, I'll never be able to understand

9

it," Sudi later lamented to me during a dinner visit to his home. "Everything is money, money, money for them. Is there no value placed on service to the community. Must wolf eat wolf and dog eat dog? I'll never understand it!"

A fiftyish woman, Lena Allen-Shore, her brunette hair done in a chignon, spoke in a sweet, melodic voice. She told the class of the five books she had authored: **L'Orage Dans Mon Coeur, Le Pain de la Pais, Ne Me Demandez Pas Qui Je Suis, May The Flowers Grow,** and **La Langue Universelle.** She also noted her poetry written for posters manufactured in California, the dramatic, panoramic kind where a young man and woman, seen only as silhouettes, walk hand in hand on a beach toward a nebulous, throbbing, orange disc that is either sunset or Armageddon.

Phillipe Reneau spoke emotionally, sometimes elliptically, of his problems as a grade-seven teacher trying to teach Montreal poor children. He had attempted to implement progressive, educational practices but discovered that mostly what he achieved was to almost get fired.

The other students' names were Ron, Mordecai, Peter, Michelle, and Parker.

"Now for the textbooks. Supposedly, they've been ordered by the campus bookstore. I haven't been over there to see if they're in but I certainly filled out the book-order forms that McGill sent me. The two texts are...." -- I began to write in chalk on the board – "**Anti-Man Culture: Bureautechnocracy and the Schools**, by Van Cleve Morris and Charles Tesconi, Jr. They're both professors at the University of Illinois campus in Chicago. I know them both."

"**Anti-Man Culture** was published this year by the University of Illinois Press in Champaign-Urbana. I wrote a long review of this book recently that will appear soon in the journal **Education and Urban Society.** Unfortunately, this book is only in hardcover and costs $7.95."

"The second, required text is **Existentialism In Education** by Van Cleve Morris alone. It's in paper and goes for $3.95. That makes a total of $11.90 for you, plus tax. I hope that's reasonable."

"Are those U.S. prices?" Phillipe asked. I nodded. "Then that means they'll cost us more. U.S. books always cost more here."

"Hmmm. Thanks for reminding me. I noticed that when I was in Toronto." (That afternoon, I visited the McGill bookstore and found the paperback hiked to $5.95 and the hardcover upped to $12.50, representing very substantial increases indeed.)

René peered bemusedly at the titles on the board. "Just what is 'bureautechnocracy,' Professor Heath?" he asked, pronouncing the unfamiliar word uncertainly. "It's a new word for me."

"Well, to be frank," I replied, "I think they got the idea from my book, published recently, **The Politics That Impede Change In The Technoversity.**" I flung my arms wide in vast disgust. "I elaborated for them, basically what they have now published themselves. I use their book here because it is shorter and cheaper and fits much better the needs of a philosophy of education class. But I wanted you to know the background here. And I promise you by the end of the class you will know the full and complete meaning of the term 'bureautechnocracy,' and all its ramifications...

"As you might infer from the titles of the texts, this course will have a lot to do with the philosophy known as existentialism. Unlike most philosophies, existentialism has not been around very long. Something in recent history made its development possible." I squinched my face into an intent, meditative expression several seconds, to further engage the students. "The massive, devastating nature of modern warfare, that is the crucial variable. Existentialism virtually sprouted from the bloodshed of millions in World War One, The Great War, the one that was to end all war. The losses were staggering, without

11

G. Louis Heath, Ph.D.

historic precedent. Europe just about destroyed itself. Something had gone drastically wrong to produce such enormous violence."

"A few Europeans began to try and figure out just what had gone wrong. They could find no answers, no comfort, in the established institutions – the nation state, the universities, the family, the church, nor business and industry, and certainly not the military. None of these had prevented the violence. Some thinkers concluded that these institutions had, in fact, **caused** the violence – certainly then a radical thought. They claimed the pre-WWI values were no longer adequate to guarantee society's survival. These were the existentialists. They maintained that the individual was all-important and that the individual had to forget society's institutions and strike out on his own. He had to create his own values and define his own existence – not let the society do it for him. It is a desperate, lonely philosophy, I think, this rejection of society, but when you view the context in which it emerged, you can begin to understand it."

I went on to analyze the Vietnam War protest movement from an existential perspective and sketch the basic views of three important existentialist philosophers: Soren Kierkegaard, the misunderstood Dane, and the pre-eminent French existentialists, Albert Camus and Jean-Paul Sartre. Then I adjourned class for the day.

Everyone beat a hasty retreat down the hall toward the exit, not as a pack, but singly and in pairs. They flung the doors open so enthusiastically that I suspected they didn't give a fig about existentialism.

I was soon outside myself, enjoying the glorious day. I shook off my philosopher pose, a lofty, insouciant expression directed obliquely upward from an obliviously tilted-forward torso, and walked briskly toward Pine Avenue House.

My best friend at Pine Avenue House that summer was Ron Reid, a third-year, McGill medical student who worked at the

12

Royal Victoria Hospital nearby. We lived on the same hall and had an opportunity to go out for a lot of good times together.

Ron hated Québec. He was there only to attend McGill University Medical School, perhaps the best in Canada. He spent a lot of time complaining about "La Belle Province," which he often referred to as "this damn province." "I can hardly wait to get out of here," he would say. "I want to go back to Alberta and practice in a small town. This Frenchie stuff is a lot of crap. The taxes are too high here and everyone's rude, and besides, I don't speak French. I can tell you this: the day I graduate, I'm driving out of here. My car will be parked and pointed west while I'm at the commencement. Once I have that M.D. degree in hand, I'm gonna jump in my car and roll!"

I would nod and smile from time to time as he worked Québec out of his system. If I ignored his anti-French crassness, he could be enormously funny.

One topic Ron especially liked to hold forth on was himself. One interesting part of his past was the time he spent in prison. He and several other eighteen-year-olds had gotten roaring drunk one night and had stolen a car. They joyrode a few hours, winding up at an Alberta provincial park, where they disassembled their pilfered means of conveyance. The next morning, the Mounties found the band of thieves asleep alfresco on and around seat cushions, fenders, the engine, and doors. Though Ron vehemently denied he had in any way consorted with the thieves, that he just happened to be sleeping near them, he was arrested with them, convicted, and sent to the penitentiary for a year, as were they all. As his cell door clanged shut the day he was first incarcerated, Ron was still loudly protesting, "The Mounties got the wrong man!," to which his guard sneered, "The Mounties always get their man!"

"The year in the pen was good for me," acknowledged Ron philosophically. "It got my life turned in the right direction when I had been going the wrong way a long time." He cracked a huge grin. "The only thing I didn't like were the Friday night movies. They always featured beautiful women like Marilyn Monroe, Sophia Loren, or the James Bond double-0-seven girls, cuz that's what the guys wanted. It sure was hell in there after one of those movies. The beds in the cellblock would squeak till four or five in the morning with violent masturbating. I never heard such loud squeaking! It sounded like a million Canadian geese taking flight. Most everyone seemed to be jerking off until he fell asleep from exhaustion. The noise was unbelievable. Sometimes I didn't get to sleep at all Friday night."

One warm, azure, Saturday afternoon, Ron and I took a drive around the island of Montreal (the city is located on a huge island in the St. Lawrence River), stopping every mile or so at a different pub. Ron made a point of saving his empty beer bottles, most of them bearing Molson and Moosehead labels. When we came upon a roadside mailbox lettered with a French name, he would fling a bottle in a high arc out of the car at the mailbox. Usually, he misfired, and it landed on the lawn behind the box. "Take that, Frenchie!" he would yell as I tried to hunch down and become invisible.

"Why do you have to do this?" I asked in exasperation. "You don't even know these people! How can you hate them?"

"I don't hate them," he retorted. "I just want to give the pea-soupers a free beer bottle."

All told, Ron hurled eighteen bottles at French mailboxes. Finally, a policeman pulled us over and asked if we knew anything about a bottle thrower in the vicinity. Ron smiled toothily and measured his words magnificently, hiding well the fact that he was drunk. "No sir, we never saw them. I mean him. I hope you get him though because anybody who'd do that sort of thing is really the lowest form of life, eh?"

The officer looked at us severely and said in a harsh, accusatory tone, "**They** certainly are!"

14

Fortunately, Ron had thrown his last bottle before someone had called the police. I had been fool enough to let him override my better judgment and toss bottles, some of which had exploded on asphalt and concrete. Certainly, I would've undoubtedly been hauled in along with the "Mad Medic from Alberta," as I began calling him on our pub-hopping tour.

As we drove around the first curve after the officer had pulled us over, Ron held a fingered fist out the window, along the extended finger of which he had wedged a plastic swizzle stick featuring a fleur-de-lys (the symbol of Québec) that he had kept from one of the bars. "That's for you, Pierre!" he growled, exploding into one of his famous guffaws that split his pallid face with a quaking, mirthful, contorting orifice that seemed strangely unlike a mouth.

I want to tell one more story about Ron. It occurred at Pine Avenue House. One morning, about three, I was awoken by a loud knocking at my door followed by a strained, asthmatic voice. "I...can't...breathe!...Help!...Hel..l..l..p!"

I jumped out of bed and threw open the door. Immediately before me was Ron, bent over, cradling his sides. "It...hard ...for....me...breathe," he wheezed. "Fraid...I...pass...out."

This was the funniest practical joke I'd ever been the brunt of! It just cracked me up. I laughed so long and hard that I doubled over and had to hold my sides to relieve the pain. Yes, **pain**. I was literally in pain from the hilarious impact of Ron's prank.

Finally, I replied with a put-on gesture of my own. I managed to cup a hand to my ear, and, through paroxysms of uncontrolled laughter, got out the Canadianism, "eh?" It was all so funny, both of us doubled over at the doorsill, racked with mirth we could not control!

Then Ron fell on the floor and couldn't get up and I knew I had a real crisis on my hands. I pulled Ron up -- he was conscious -- and hauled him to my car, where I carefully positioned him onto his back in the backseat. Quickly, I drove off toward the Royal Victoria Hospital.

By the time we got to the hospital, Ron was feeling a little better and he said he'd rather wait a while before he went to the emergency room. "Let's go to the canteen," he suggested, beckoning me toward the 24-hour facility. "I don't want to be embarrassed by sounding a false alarm. I often get these attacks, but I thought this time I really was gonna die. At least for a while there."

Ron bought a coffee from a machine and poured five or six packets of sugar into it. "I hope that makes you feel better," I chided. "I hope your doctor prescribed sugar for you."

Ron flashed a smile that was about half its usual wattage. "The best damn doctor in La Belle Province prescribed this concoction," he said defiantly. His voice had steadied and I could tell he was feeling better. He was beginning to sound like an asshole again.

About five a.m., Ron told me to go on home alone, that he would stick at the canteen a while longer to be sure his attack was over. I had a cup of soup out of a vending machine and returned home to bed.

Ron never mentioned what caused his attacks, if he ever knew. I think that his seizure, at least its severity, may have been linked to his working two shifts as an extern at the "Royal Vic" the entire summer. The seizure occurred in late August after he had looked wan and haggard most the month. He had complained the day of the attack about not getting enough sleep as he left Pine Avenue House for a second shift after only four hours off-duty.

About a year after I left Montreal, I received a letter from Ron dated October 11, 1973. He had married a young woman who had recently immigrated to Canada from Lyons, France. "She is not stuck up about being a University of Lyons graduate," he wrote from Montreal, "nor has she ever let me down. I am very happy."

I thought wryly that luckily for Ron his bride had agreed to the convention that the wife takes the man's name. Otherwise, Ron's own mailbox would never have survived the frequent explosions of his own airborne, empty, beer bottles!

During the first week of my philosophy class, one student said absolutely nothing. He even declined to introduce himself the first day. He was Mordecai.

In a small seminar, it is a serious pedagogical error to allow anyone to sit as a spectator. Therefore, on Friday, the fourth day of class, I attempted to draw Mordecai into the discussion, questioning him about an assigned reading I had put on reserve in the library. "Mordecai, I'd be very much interested in how you interpret Miguel de Unamuno's existentialist term 'the tragic sense of life'?"

Thank goodness I asked the question near the end of class. Mordecai compressed his lips and hung his head as a crimson glow spread over his throat and face. He was clearly very embarrassed, to state the obvious, and everyone was made ill-at-ease. I was delighted when someone intervened and volunteered an answer to the question. A short discussion followed and then I adjourned the class. I could hear a subdued, collective sigh of relief.

I'll get Mordecai involved later, I thought. Maybe I'll have him into my office to discuss how we can do that. But Mordecai did not appear at the next class on Monday, nor for a long time. In fact, he did not show up again till the very last day of the six-week course. The class had forgotten him, but there he sat, over a month later, grim and stoic, as we discussed the last seminar paper, "The Philosophy of Heidegger: Its Educational Implications For The West-End Montreal Schools."

Mordecai's forbidding, concrete-like façade dampened a bit our mutual joy over nearing the end of the course. Yet, Mordecai aside, it was a great meeting. The last paper was compelling and provoked lively discussion. Everyone, save Mordecai, was pleasant and in high spirits. And the class had come up with an excellent cap-off for the course. On behalf of the class, Lena stood up and presented me with a gold tie tack engraved with three, tiny fleurs-de-lys. She shook my hand and kissed me on the cheek. She then gave me an inscribed copy of her book **La Langue Universelle**, reading her words aloud from the title page. "To Dr. G. Louis Heath – Your words help us to believe that one day the flowers will grow in the gardens of humanity. Lena Allen-Shore." The other students' signatures appeared below hers.

After class, I turned toward the inscrutable Mordecai. "Can I speak with you a few minutes?" he asked meekly.

"Certainly," I replied. "Why don't we walk downtown and talk over a cup of coffee. I want to get out of this building. It's so nice outside."

Mordecai nodded and followed me out the building with the downcast air of a hockey player who had just lost a game to the Soviets.

We walked down the mountain along McTavish Street. As we passed the faculty club, Mordecai began to talk. "I'm sorry I haven't attended your class," he apologized, his voice trailing off.

"Why were you absent so much?"

"It's sort of complex, Dr. Heath. D'you remember the question you asked me the first week?" I nodded. "Well, y'see, I just wasn't ready for that. When I signed up for your class, I thought it would be larger, at least twenty or so, so that I could just listen and take notes, eh?" I nodded again. "Well, I'm not the kind to speak in small groups. I'm a nervous person and that sort of thing bothers me." Mordecai looked at me briefly with a woebegone expression. There was a beseeching quality to the sadness in his eyes that gave me the impression that this young man could well be in psychological hot water – not deep, but deep enough to cause distress.

"You should've told me that at the beginning, Mordecai. I wouldn't have asked you another question the whole class if you'd told me your wishes," I said in a sympathetic voice.

Mordecai drooped his head. "Yeah, I guess I shoulda. But I'm not very smart in things like that. Just too shy I guess."

The pathos of this guy was just killing me. He was as klutzy about classroom matters as I am in the arcane and internecine world of academic politics. "What I can't understand, Mordecai, is why you're showing up again today, at, of all times, the last day of class?"

Mordecai raised his head and set his jaw as if about to take a blow. "I guess I came to make a desperate plea…"

"You guess?" I chimed in.

"**I know** I came to make a desperate plea," he amended. "I want to ask you to please let me do a paper for credit in your course. This is my only course this summer and I want to go back to California with something to show for it. I don't want to blow it simply because I'm afraid to talk in class."

"California? I thought you were from Québec?"

"Well, I'm part from Québec, part from California, and part from Israel."

I gave Mordecai an offended, I've-been-had look. "Holy shit and kiss my ass. It just had to be me! You're a CIA triple agent!" I jested in a serious, exasperated tone.

"No, just a student," returned Mordecai timidly.

My eyebrows arched up. "Then please tell me how you're from three places at once. No, wait, stop. Wait here. I wanna buy today's **Le Devoir**." I popped into the Metropolitan News And Tobacco Shop, plunked down twenty cents, and popped out with a paper. "Let's see. Where were we?"

Mordecai emitted the faintest hint of a smile. "CIA."

"Oh yes. C is for Canadian childhood in Montreal. I is for Israel. Shalom! And A is for Angeleno and absent." I peered intently at Mordecai. "Did this **choochem** professor miss anything?"

Mordecai's lips twitched nervously into another fleeting, subtle smile and he shook his head. I liked the fellow. I could tell he wasn't trying to kiss my professional ass. An ingenuous fellow. In fact, I was rather disarmed by his candor. Most students grade out around 75 to 80 percent bullshit, chickenshit, or horseshit, or some mixture of the three, but this guy didn't seem to be any kind of B.S., C.S., or H.S. artist. "OK now," I continued, "tell me more about the CIA. Begin with I and A. I'm dying to hear."

Mordecai made eye contact with me, something he'd been largely avoiding. "Well, the I is for Israel. My mother lives in Israel and I visit her as often as I can. I also lived in Tel Aviv near her for three years. I'm Jewish, of course."

"I surmise that since you grew up in Montreal, Canada, the C, that your mother moved to the I, Israel, not terribly long ago?"

"Six years ago. She got scared of Québec. Too many labor strikes and too much violence and separatism for her. I got scared, too. That's when I decided to transfer from McGill to UCLA."

"Ah, so that's where you want to transfer credit."

"No. I didn't stay at UCLA long, only a semester. The student demonstrations there, I hated them. Wherever there is disruption like that, the Jews will get it, sooner or later. So, I transferred to a small Catholic college. I like it better."

"Ah, very interesting." We had by this time crossed Sherbrooke Avenue, passed Ben's Delicatessen, and were walking along Ste. Catherine Street. I grabbed Mordecai lightly by the arm. "In here. Let's have our coffee in Brasserie Le Tramway. It's a good place." Like a fool, I added, "I'm buying."

Once we had seated ourselves, I asked, "D'you want something to eat too, Mordecai?" I have now, I kicked myself mentally, carried secular humanism far too far.

"Well, yes, maybe a sandwich or something, but only if I can pay." Mordecai seemed a bit embarrassed.

"Oh but it will be my honor to allow you to pay," I rejoined. "Waitress! Waitress!" A pert, twentyish waitress several booths away looked my way. "We wanna order!" She approached, smiling with that unctuous sincerity that is downtown Montreal's trademark, and took our order. Our coffee and sandwiches were soon before us.

Mordecai and I sipped our too-hot coffee and peered at each other – I directly, Mordecai furtively – over the rims of our cups as though they were barricades, the eternal barriers between teacher and student. A René Simard song began to play on the juke box. "Let's get this term paper thing out of the way, shall we?" Mordecai's eyes became alert and bore intently in on me as I began to speak in my class-meeting voice. "Well now," I said, clearing my throat portentously, "you've invested almost no time and, as far as I'm concerned, too much tuition in this course. It does pain me greatly that you missed most the lectures and discussions. They were a great learning experience for all, including me. But we can't worry about the hockey puck that got away, can we?" Mordecai gave a half-nod. "The question becomes, Mordecai, how can I save your ass at the eleventh hour and still satisfy myself that you have learned enough to justify a passing grade?" Mordecai gave a third of a nod. "You seem willing enough, and, I would guess, able enough, to benefit from an alternative course requirement. So this is what I want: why don't you do a paper twice as long as I required of the other students?" Mordecai's eyes lit up. "That would be sixty pages. **But**, your paper must be very high in quality for me to give you the equivalent of a C." (In 1972, McGill gave percentage grades.) "To do otherwise wouldn't be fair to the students who put up with my Yankee iconoclasm and cynicism every day. We aren't running a correspondence school here, y'know?"

Mordecai seemed grateful as well as relieved. "That's fine, very good. Thank you. Thank you very much," he emoted, in his first departure from the wooden and laconic. "I really, **really**, appreciate this."

Mordecai exited Brasserie Le Tramway comporting himself with a less rigid posture and walking with a more relaxed gait than he had displayed upon entering. Knowing he could export credit from Québec to California had apparently removed a great burden from his shoulders. He seemed to stride ahead with a new resolution and confidence, helped along no doubt by the pastrami sandwich that was beginning to release energy into his bloodstream.

Just before I left Montreal, over two months later, Mordecai's 61-page term paper arrived by first-class mail, postmarked Salt Lake City, Utah. Mordecai had evidently mailed his tome en route back to Los Angeles.

I had to go to the post office to get the paper. Forty-two cents' postage was due. For sure the thing wasn't worth 42 cents, but it was worth a C-. It was a well-researched paper comparing Martin Buber's philosophy to that of Kierkegaard and the educational implications thereof. The major flaw was that it took a new and unpredictable turn every four or five pages. Its vagaries seemed to say as much about the enigmatic Mordecai as it did about the mysteries of existentialist educational philosophy.

Wherever you are, Mordecai, you **trumbenyick**, I hope you read this and send me the 42 cents you owe me, which, adjusted for inflation, comes to exactly $15,000 U.S.

The only truly memorable faculty acquaintance I made at McGill was one I shall call "Winston." I didn't meet him in the faculty lounge until late in the summer.

Winston, about 45, was one of those peripatetic academics. He had made a career of teaching two and three years here and there in North America and around the world. He had been at McGill two years.

Just before I returned to Illinois State University, we got together for lunch at the Kon-Tiki Restaurant in the downtown Sheraton Hotel to talk about this and that, two professionals breaking bread and sparkling together over intellectual matters. At least that's what I thought the lunch was for.

I had no more than nibbled at my shrimp salad than Winston began to tell me of his inner turmoil and the details of his plan to commit suicide. The man was suffering an acute career crisis. "If I don't get tenure at McGill," he averred, "I'll use my suicide plan. I'll commit suicide for sure then, but I may commit suicide before that because I just **know** they're going to ask me to leave." His face assumed an even more distressed appearance. "I'm a failure, can't you see? I've been all over the world but don't have a university to call home. I'm a middle-aged failure, a has-been, a never-was!"

Winston went on to tell me of the disastrous relationship he'd just ended with a woman Ph.D. candidate in English. As he did so, it struck me as obvious that the cumulative effect of not putting down roots somewhere, his sense of failure, and the collapse of his recent love life had brought him to the brink. Being a lovelorn failure without a country to call home -- though he was an American citizen -- will do it every time. And I wondered why in the world he'd picked me to unburden himself. "Why are you telling me all this?" I asked.

Winston's gimlet eyes fixed on me. "Because I can't talk with any of the permanent people at McGill," he said in an edgy voice building in tension. "You're visiting. You'll be leaving soon. I feel I can trust you." Winston was on the verge of crying.

"I see, but I can't see why you want to kill yourself," I said in a soothing tone. "You seem to have a nice life as a professor. You come from a wealthy family. You're educated. You've seen the world. You're only in your forties." I paused thoughtfully. "If I had it as good as you, I wouldn't think of suicide. I'd go out and celebrate."

Winston studied me, saying nothing a weighty few seconds. "Yes, yes, yes," he finally said excitedly. "I knew you might try to talk me out of killing myself, but I know from what they say about you around the department that you are a compassionate person, a good listener. I need someone like you to talk to who won't go and blab and get me fired for just talking."

So, I listened a full two hours until my shrimp shriveled up and my lettuce wilted. Winston recounted his past and his problems: the women who had blighted his life, the department chairmen who had shafted him, the culture shocks he'd suffered moving about the world, and his wealthy parents who expected too much of him. "I never married," he confided in a voice tremulous with emotion, "because I wanted to achieve something significant first to satisfy my parents. I failed!"

Winston put the perfect ending to the lunch by describing the fine points of his planned suicide.

About 2:30 p.m., we at last left the Kon-Tiki and walked to the edge of campus. Winston grabbed my hand and shook it frenetically. "Thank you for listening to me. I appreciate it!" We then went our separate ways.

I never heard whether Winston killed himself.

The neighborhood north of McGill, an area of substandard housing known as Milton-Park, faced a grim future the summer of 1972. The city had condemned it and hired Concordia Estates, a high-rise development corporation, to tear it down, and build vaulting, glistening structures of ferroconcrete. T-booms and bulldozers had begun to work, collapsing Milton-Park's ancient, historic frame houses and tall mansions with the dispassionate efficiency of a highly mechanized army crushing a peasant uprising.

I often walked through Milton-Park. I became an observer of the transformation going on. It saddened me to see the old, Victorian-style homes crumble into rubble and their remains carried off. They were certainly unsafe to live in, some of them anyway, but I kept thinking how much better -- though less profitable? -- it would be to renovate the old homes, preserving them as residences as well as charming, architectural timepieces. Demolishing them struck me as akin to killing the last of a species, as thoroughly avaricious and inexcusable. Thus, the clangor and rataplan of the wrecking machines especially irritated me.

Most the businesses in Milton-Park had been sold. They stood boarded up and drearily lifeless. Yet, there were two inspiring holdouts to the "progress" under way. They were Tabagie Arsenault and the Oriental Pastry Shop, the last symbols of stability in a world that was literally falling down.

Tabagie Arsenault, a newspaper, tobacco, and novelty shop, was located on Park Avenue. I regularly bought a paper there and a pastry at the nearby Oriental, and sat on a bench in the sun to read and munch in the august presence of Victorian and Edwardian architecture. I knew that I would never enjoy doing this in the shadow of the tall, ferroconcrete monsters that were to supplant it. To be blunt, I don't find such material and technological newness very impressive. That's why the U.S. space program turns me off. I can only think about the "slums" like Milton-Park that could have been restored or the hungry kids on Indian reservations that could be fed.

The Arsenault shop had been a focal point of life in Milton-Park for over a half century. A dour man in his late seventies ran the shop, assisted by an obese, calico cat who slept and shed hair on the stacks of newspapers. The proprietor had survived Vimy in World War I. Concordia's bulldozers – he called them "tanks" – seemed a minor nuisance to him vis-à-vis the gas and shelling of The Great War which remained sharp in his memory.

"The Anglo bastards are coming!" he told me in English with a French accent. "They will have to bury me alive! I won't give that pack of wolves the satisfaction of moving!" He pulled out a musty, beribboned, bronze medal, crusty with a heavy cast. "I will earn this again if I have to!" he vowed defiantly. "The Anglo-Canadian wolves will never chew me up!"

A stooped, wizened, Chinese couple in their late sixties owned the Oriental Pastry Shop. They seemed to be in poor health, but my first impression proved deceiving, for they were, in fact, quite healthy, working long hours and not suffering unduly for it. The secret they said was that they ate little pastry, sticking to a diet rich in vegetables, fish, and rice. "I never eat this junk!" the man exclaimed. "It will kill you if you eat too much. It is junk food." His wife smiled broadly behind him, either in agreement or amusement.

The Milton-Park residents, mostly students and old people who had been protesting the demolitions long before they began, put their resistance into high gear while I was at McGill. They organized a loosely-knit group called the Milton-Park Citizens Committee that sponsored street demonstrations the last weekend of August. Some 100 residents, including a good number of McGill students, marched along Prince Arthur Street with signs bearing messages such as "Houses Are For Living In," "People Live Here," "Evict Concordia," and "Professor Heath Loves You, Milton-Park!" -- the last, of course, my sign, and a damn good one, made of tagboard with the words inked on in superb, Gothic script.

We demonstrators sang some of the standard protest songs that had been popularized or written by the likes of Bob Dylan, Joan Baez, Malvina Reynolds, and Pete Seeger, as we walked in several compact circles on the street. After four hours of this, a policeman came by to remind us that our parade permit would expire in a few minutes, at 4 p.m. I could have kissed that officer, my feet ached so terribly!

I hustled back to Pine Avenue House where I shaved my scruffy, five-day beard off and changed out of my hippie outfit. The long-haired wig, the Indian headband, the leather vest, the hemp sandals, and the stinky blue jeans all went back to the thrift store where I'd bought them. In exchange, they gave me a small library of used books, including a great French-Canadian one, Gabrielle Roy's **The Tin Flute**, which made excellent reading fare the remainder of the summer.

From Montreal, I observed Canadian nationalism at work by following events in Alberta through the media. The Calgary city council had hired Oakland, California police chief Charles Gain as its new top cop by a six to five vote. However, massive popular resentment against the appointment soon built up. Letters and phone calls deluged city hall. When Mayor Rod Sykes escorted Gain into the city council chamber to formally present the new incumbent, protestors chanted "Yankee Go Home" and bristled signs with such messages as "Keep It Canadian," "Is This The 51st State?" and, "Porky Pig Is An American, Eh?" The overflow crowd derisively hummed "The Star-Spangled Banner" off-key and theatrically waved miniature American flags as if to greet a conquering army.

The hiring of Gain in Calgary struck me immediately as immensely ridiculous. I wasn't fully aware then of Canada's record of hiring so many Americans for choice jobs, including a lot of tenurable, university positions. I had assumed that anyone who served permanently as a policeman or professor had to be a Canadian citizen. It was a poor assumption on my part, I admit, because most of the faculty I had met at the Ontario Institute for Studies in Education and at McGill were Americans. I should have been more perceptive and begun with the opposite assumption.

Police Chief Gain must have gotten the message because he soon resigned. I guess he felt he couldn't be as effective as he wished, nor as comfortable. I and other Americans, not only Gain, had been given notice: qualified Canadians would be hired first, especially for positions like police chief where a Canadian ought obviously to be.

The hire-qualified-Canadians-first policy touched all my summer appointments. Each job I got, usually six weeks in duration, was advertised throughout Canada. In each instance, the administrator who hired me had to certify in a letter to the provincial minister of education that I was the most qualified candidate. On two applications, I lost out to superior Canadian competition (at Mount Allison University in 1973 and at the

27

University of Toronto in 1974), although I was fortunate enough to be hired elsewhere one of those summers (the University of British Columbia, 1973).

A cadaverous, drab creature lived on my floor at Pine Avenue House. She was a German-Canadian lady in her eighties known as "Frau Rommel." She always wore the same, dreary, brown housedress from which the pattern had long since faded save for small, faint patches on the sleeves. Frau Rommel reminded me of a greatly wrinkled, dried apricot, wrapped in a cured, light-brown tobacco leaf and topped by a much-used mophead dyed gray.

The emaciated, old frump talked and sang incessantly to herself in German, filling the corridor with dark mutterings and shrill, off-key lyrics as she moved stealthily to and from the hallway bathroom, which she monopolized to the chagrin of the other floor residents. She locked herself in a good dozen times a day and took an inordinate amount of time on each occasion with her ablutions or whatever she did in there. I could hear much weeping and sobbing interpolated into the toilet conversations she had with herself in her screeching, discordant voice. If I knocked, she would scream an incoherent, hyena-like reply. I soon didn't bother to knock when I knew she was inside. It wasn't worth the pain.

Most the time, I gave up on my floor's bathroom and took my business to the one upstairs, a practice followed by most who lived on Frau Rommel's floor. Like refugees everywhere, we rapidly became **personae non gratae** upstairs despite the widespread knowledge that the "crazy old lady" was a vexation to us. So, we extended our visits up another floor in what some joker called "Operation Manure Spreader." This vertical fertilization didn't exactly thin out our visits enough to make us popular, but at least no one floor regarded us as public health hazard number one.

I should acknowledge that I offered to sell my fellow residents portable potty chairs for their rooms. The Canadians told me in the strongest language that I was just another American trying to capitalize on human misery. I told them to go potty wherever they saw fit, that theirs was a free country.

Frau Rommel was found dead in her room in early September, sprawled in a grotesque position across her covers-mussed bed, her swollen, black tongue beetling out between her blood-caked, clenched teeth. An empty pill bottle was frozen into her right hand. Beside her on the nightstand lay a brief suicide note penned in an ornate, slightly scrawled script.

I was called on to examine the note by the almost hysterical cleaning lady who found the body. My German is touristy, owing to but a single semester at Berkeley, but I was able to piece together that Frau Rommel wished her remains returned to Germany for burial. Later translations by someone proficient in the language added the information that Frau Rommel wanted to be interred beside her six sons who had died fighting in the German army.

Everyone felt saddened by Frau Rommel's death. It might not have happened, we thought, had she been in a nursing home with proper care instead of being forced to fend for herself in the Hobbesian world of a rooming house.

The arrival of the National League-leading Cincinnati Reds' baseball team in mid-August to play the Montreal Expos gave me an opportunity to get together with my old friend, pitcher Gary Nolan. We had grown up together in the Sierra foothills, in Oroville, California, near the local baseball diamond where Nolan, I, and my brother Larry regularly practiced baseball.

I called the Queen Elizabeth Hotel where the Reds stayed and got Nolan's roommate, another pitcher, who jested, "Gary's in the shower with fourteen French women. They won't take off their clothes, he's so ugly." This was the most intellectually substantial comment I was to hear from a Cincinnati ballplayer (except for Nolan, who is uncommonly articulate and poised for a ball player without a day of higher education under his belt).

A few minutes later I called back and got Gary Nolan. Since I couldn't hear any French spoken in the background, I inferred that he'd dismissed the fourteen women. "It's great to hear from you, Gary," Nolan enthused. (We share the name, Gary.) "Whereya at? Is this long distance?"

"No, I'm here in Montreal."

"Montreal!"

"Yes, right here in Montreal. I've been teaching at McGill University."

"My Gill? Never heard of it. Is it part of My Fish University?" he chortled.

"No. They're in no way affiliated...Frankly, Gary, you know damn well there is no such thing as My Fish University." I came to the point with Nolan. "I'd like to get together with you. Is that possible?"

"It sure is. I wouldn't miss seeing you for a World Series ring."

"Where do I meet you?"

"In the lobby by the registration desk. I'll be there just before noon. You can have a meal on the club, then go on the bus with us to Jarry Park. I'll get a ticket for you."

"Sounds great. I'll be there. I never ate with a pro ball club before."

"See you just before noon."

"Right on, all-star," I said as I hung up. My use of "all-star" referred to Nolan's selection for the annual National League-versus-American League All-Star Game that had been played over a month earlier. Unfortunately, due to arm trouble, Nolan hadn't been able to participate, nor had he since pitched in regular-season games for the same reason.

I was pleased to be invited to dine with the Reds. I looked forward to it. I, the unknown Ph.D. making a lot less than Nolan's $60,000 -- those were the days just before free agency -- was about to mingle with world-famous sports celebrities pulling down huge salaries. The prospect was enough to put things in perspective, conveying me out of a world where books and ideas reign supreme to one of high commercial success.

Nolan barely managed to graduate from Oroville High School, where I had graduated first in my class. Yet, after long years of further, assiduous study -- B.A., M.A., Ph.D. -- I was the cipher and Nolan the star. Back home in Northern California, when I said I was from Oroville, I often got the response, "Oh, that's where that famous pitcher Gary Nolan's from!" This awareness owed to media coverage of the Oroville fans who regularly traveled in bus caravans to the games Nolan pitched against the San Francisco Giants. The Oroville people went in droves to watch their hero strike out the likes of Willie Mays and Willie McCovey. I took one of those buses in 1968 while I was working on my doctorate at Berkeley. Some **schmendrick** came up and asked me if I had moved my shoe store from downtown Oroville out to the new shopping plaza. He had me confused with someone. I told the idiot where I would put both my shoes, plus my jacket and cap, if he didn't return to his seat.

I walked downtown to the Queen Elizabeth Hotel and found Nolan in the lobby right off. He was dressed in burgundy blazer and open-necked sport shirt, and smiling. "It's good to seeya, Gary!" he greeted.

"Long time, no see," I replied. "The last time was in Oroville."

Nolan nodded and led me into the dining room where we seated ourselves at a small table. At a larger table nearby I recognized superstars Johnny Bench and Pete Rose who were definitely looking at me, hoping Nolan would introduce me to them. I soon realized, however, that they were ogling the very attractive waitress in the background behind me, and that I just happened to be in the way. So, I quickly removed the pleased, expectant expression I had on and tried not to betray the fact that I felt more than a little embarrassed.

The white-haired manager, Sparky Anderson, was seated on the far side of the restaurant with his coaches and a middle-aged fellow in a business suit. César Geronimo, who sat with a black player and two other Hispanics -- the minority table, I thought -- was the only other Red I recognized as I cursorily surveyed the room. Many of them were national heroes, popular icons, though not particularly mine. Would they recognize my heroes and icons, sociologists such as Émile Durkheim and Max Weber or authors such as Harold A. Sinclair of Bloomington, Illinois and Hugh Garner of Toronto, Ontario? Of course not. They are but men who can hit, pitch, and catch baseballs. My icons are much more transcendent and enduring, although their names almost never find widespread recognition in popular culture. The Reds baseball team would have no clue as to who they are and their great importance.

I ate the most expensive item on the menu, lobster thermidor. I'd been eating primarily at the Royal Victoria Hospital cafeteria, Moshe's Steak House (whenever I attended the Verdi Movie Theatre), Ben's Delicatessen, and the McGill Student Union the entire summer. I was determined to take advantage of this opportunity for free, four-star cuisine at the Queen Elizabeth. With my meal, I imbibed a couple glasses of excellent Riesling wine, a decided contrast to the fruity Gallo I kept in my room. Nolan ate a steak and drank iced tea, totally unaware that he had taken on board a refugee from Pine Avenue House, a place where all the rodents were larger than baseballs and some were bigger than Johnny Bench's catcher's mitt and a lot more menacing, too.

As we dined, I pointed to Nolan's pitching arm, his right. "Just what's the problem with your arm? Is it serious?"

Nolan shook his head. "No, not serious, but it could be if I let 'em horse me into pitching too soon, which is what they've been trying to do. I just tell 'em I'm not ready. I won't cave in." Nolan lowered his voice and spoke in a confidential tone so that Pete Rose and Johnny Bench couldn't hear. "Listen, Gary, you gotta watch out for number one in this business. You're just another horse to them, see. They wanna get all they can out of ya, so they'll push you when you're not ready if you let them. Leaving baseball is quicker than death, so you've gotta take care of your health all the time. They're guys who are on the top a year or two and then suddenly they're gone. They can't even make the minors. They don't see it coming and they leave baseball without a dime."

I nodded absently, absorbed in his message.

"I don't want that to happen to me," he continued. "I wanna last ten years so I can leave with something. I have kids and a wife to take care of, y'know. I gotta think of them. I can't go out and do a fool thing like pitch in the All-Star Game when my arm is sore just because it's such a big honor and it goes to my head. That could be the end, right there! Nosirree. I'll just take my own sweet time nursing my wing back to health and when I know I'm ready I'll be out there pitching, and no sooner. I made one comeback from a bad arm and I can do it again."

"I'm all for you," I commiserated. "I don't want to see you sent down to the minors again."

I tried to get Nolan off the subject of baseball at one point in the conversation. I told him about the Québec Liberation Front, the FLQ, and its terrorist activities in Montreal and how they had kidnapped two officials, Michael Cross and Pierre LaPorte, murdering the latter. I could tell Nolan was only being polite by pretending to be interested in what I said. He'd never heard of the FLQ, separatism, Le Parti Québecois, or even the antipathy between Québec and English Canada. When I'd finished my tidy little summary of recent Québec history that I had been absorbed in all summer, Nolan stared at me and finally he said, with the air that it was high time he said **something**, "I'll be a son of a bitch, if that doesn't beat all."

We talked about my M.D. brother Larry who was Nolan's catcher in high school and who had caught for the Stanford University baseball team that won a NCAA title. Glancing furtively at Johnny Bench at the next table, he intoned **sotto**

33

voce, "I think Larry was a better catcher than Johnny Bench. I really do."

I smiled, pleased to hear the accolade for my brother. "It was either go to medical school or go to Vietnam," I lamented. "I know he feels an empty spot inside him that will always be there because he could not go on and find out how good he might have become."

We wound up our conversation by talking about our parents who still lived in Oroville. "Thank your father for letting me borrow his pickup the last time I was home," said Nolan.

"I'll do that," I promised.

On the team bus we sat behind Johnny Bench and Pete Rose who talked the entire trip to the ball park about stock and bond investments.

After the game, which the Reds won, I waited for Nolan at the players' exit. Several, attractive, young women were also waiting. Most were unknown to the players but two were immediately embraced and kissed by a pair of Reds, an infielder and an outfielder, who escorted the mini-skirted, glossy-lipped French women to a car and drove off.

Nolan and I made our way to a nearby brasserie and had a beer, over which Nolan told me of the recent, untimely death of Reds' player Chico Ruiz and his well-attended funeral. "It just tore me up," he said sadly. Then we told each other several bawdy jokes and laughed till our sides ached.

Today, Gary Nolan is a highly paid "pit boss" for a Las Vegas casino. He supervises a sector of the floor gambling operation and does PR that capitalizes on the fact that a lot of people still remember him or at least can be informed what he once was, a pitcher who lasted over a decade in major league baseball with a lifetime 110-70 won-lost record and who pitched in two World Series and even hit a World Series home run.

Gary Heath, Ph.D., has yet to be known, and therefore cannot be remembered. He remains a cipher, who draws a monthly pension check from Illinois State University and now teaches at Mount St. Clare College in Clinton, Iowa, about the finest place, I sincerely believe, for an undergraduate to study that one can find. Big state universities are fine and have their place. Illinois State University has many outstanding teachers and the students are wonderful. But at tiny Mount St. Clare, enrollment about 600, we are a teaching family engaged in an important mission. We all feel that specialness, that sense of dedicated community, and it brings out the best in us all, both as teachers and as people. Our students are the beneficiaries.

That summer in Montreal, Team Canada began an historic eight-game hockey series against the Soviet Union. I bought a ticket for the first game, expecting the Canadians to trounce the unheralded Red Central Army team. After all, the **Montreal Star** had smugly predicted victory with the headline, "Team Canada In Four!" and I had grown up believing the Canadians were invincible in hockey. I counted on Canada winning the opener with the same confidence that I look east for sunrise and west for sunset.

I composed the following doggerel prior to the game to express my attitude:

Who's this Soviet goalie? Vladislav Tretiak's his name.
He thinks he can come over here and play **our** game.
Twenty years old, he's only a child.
Really! This is more than should be allowed.
And this Valery Kharlamov, the forward, who's he?
Can he slip one by Ken Dryden, Team Canada's goalie?
How can these unknowns oppose our Phil Esposito?
Against our Wayne Cashman, what can they do?
We'll body-check the Red Army into the ice!
Violence against the boards, that'll suffice.

The symbol of our national honor is the hockey puck.
How can these Soviet buggers have any luck?
We predict Team Canada will lose not one!
We'll win four straight, have lots of fun!

Game One: I sat far above the ice, near the rafters, between a middle-aged electrical engineer, Ted, and a retired naval officer, Dennis, from Saskatchewan, the origin of most Canadian navy men I met. The three of us got to talking before the game and concluded that Team Canada would win by at least five goals. We even expressed sympathy for the poor Soviets who should've known better than agree to a protracted eight-game series (four played in different Canadian cities, beginning with Montreal, and four in different Soviet cities).

Dennis opined, "I don't know why they're even holding this series. To give the Russians hockey lessons I guess. There's no way the Soviet amateurs can compete with our pros." He curled his lips into a pained expression. "The poor buggers," he winced. "I hate the Communists but I feel sorry for 'em tonight. It's like sending 'em to slaughter!"

Ted grinned broadly and asked, "Dennis, you should've bet on this game. I guess you didn't want to exploit the poor Soviets, eh?"

"Oh but I did bet," returned Dennis. "$100 on Team Canada to win by at least three. I thought that was safe enough since we'll win by at least five, and probably ten or fifteen, maybe even as much as twenty. It all depends on how many our players want to score."

Ted eyed Dennis critically. "Yes, but what if Team Canada decides to let up near the end and lets the Soviets score goals. Maybe they'll let them score until the margin of victory is only two! Then you've had it, eh?"

Dennis' brow furrowed and he grimaced. "Dammit. I never thought of that! Y'know, our players are such good sports, they might just do that, eh?" He slapped his forehead forcefully with the palm of his hand. "I shoulda bet less on the first game to see how much Team Canada plans to win by. I could lose a hundred dollars!"

The Canadians skated onto the ice as the crowd rose in tumultuous applause and chanted, "Team Canada! Team Canada! Team Canada!..." The chant was incessant and powerful, and its diapason rolled from the crowd out over the ice and back, again and again. The acoustics seemed ideal for their deep-throated adulation of the most exalted of national personages. The din was deafening.

"Kick the puck out of 'em, Wayne! High-stick the Communism out of 'em, Kenny! Punch 'em in the mouth, Phil!" I shouted. Messieurs Cashman, Dryden, and Esposito seemed to glance my way just a little when I called their names! They were totally drinking in the fans' rousing, reverberating support of them. They knew the fans would gladly lick the very ice they skated on had they but asked. "Team Canada! Team Canada!..." the multitude continued to iterate.

I was entranced by the powerful, nationalistic roar. I felt damn proud to be even a tiny part of that most historic, sports event. The magnitude of the event pierced to my very core. There I was, standing amid the most adoring, star-struck sports crowd I had ever observed. Yet, under the generous, voluble surface lurked a ferocious Canadian-ness, a growling, snarling spirit. I could feel their Canadian blood rising under high pressure, ready to be turned loose on the sorry Soviets. I could feel the crowd tension ripple. My corpuscles became aware first, then my person. It was that tribal, the growing sensation of confrontation between one tribe of the Cold War, the Good Guys, the Canadians, and another tribe, the Bad Guys, the guys who wore Red Stars instead of black hats.

"Team Canada looks great tonight, eh?" I bellowed over the enraptured din. I could see Prime Minister Pierre Trudeau and his wife Margaret far below, sitting in choice seats, each seemingly focussed independently on the warm-ups of the teams. They struck me as being tense in each other's presence, and I imagined I could feel that tension above the frenetic energy that

37

was rippling icy-hot through the crowd. Margaret looked stunning in a green-and-cerise paisley-patterned designer dress despite her rather sombre expression and stolid demeanor. Could it be that she was invisibly body-checking Pierre in a rather idiosyncratic, non-contact, yet highly nonverbal way?

But who was I to speculate on the tortured marriage of the Trudeaus that would later culminate in divorce? Somehow I knew already it was all over with one quick sweeping look at them across the ice.

Team Canada didn't score on their first possession, which came as something of a shock to the crowd. Nor did they score on their second or third or fourth possessions. And, when the Red Central Army team led at the end of the first period, a pall of gloomy foreboding descended upon the fans. The surface, good-natured ebullience and premature celebration had gone out of the fans like a brightly-colored party balloon deflating. A wave of embarrassment and nervousness was building in the crowd. Not even the lusty, subterranean snarl that abided in the gut of that crowd could prevent that wave from crashing hard upon us.

"This is a bit of a shock, eh?" Dennis said glumly, disbelief written on his face. "I never thought I'd live to see this."

"Cheer up, Dennis," I comforted. "Remember, your guys, our guys, haven't been playing together as a team very long. They have yet to get their act together. I'll bet they're in the locker room right now, ironing out the flaws! I guarantee you. You can look for better things in the second period. Our guys will ignite and show the Red Army a thing or two. The Reds'll wish they only came for private lessons when the final score flashes on the board above!" I pointed at the scoreboard for dramatic effect.

Dennis' face brightened a little. "I guess you're right. I guess I'm too down about all this. We know we've got the best players. I've just gotta give 'em time, eh?"

"Yes indeed, you've got the world's best," I agreed. "I expect Team Canada to get this thing turned around soon." What

I didn't say, what everybody was thinking, was that the Soviets were impressive. Their precision passing and highly disciplined play clearly surpassed the initial, lackluster performance of the Canadians. But, like everyone else, I felt the Canadians had been caught momentarily off guard by a far better team than they'd expected to take the ice against them. The Canadians would doubtless adjust and overtake the Soviets.

Yet, by the end of the second period, the Soviets retained a lead, and Dennis, Ted, and I were saying, "This is too much!"

During the intermission following the second period, Ted pontificated on the situation. "Too much rampant individualism," he observed. "Face it. Our players aren't disciplined enough. Each is out there doing his own private superstar thing while the Soviets are scoring goals." Ted pointed at a huge Labatts Beer ad on the far wall. "See there, over there!" He waggled his finger at the sign for emphasis. "Our guys usually play violent hockey, lots of body-checking and fistfights, in order to sell that beer over there, and other crap like cigarettes. This is what pays their outrageous salaries!" Ted took a thoughtful pull on his cigarette, his eyes shining intently. "It comes down to a simple thing, eh. Tonight Team Canada has run smack dab into goddam Communism. It's not a good system. People aren't happy under it. But it sure as hell is working for them out on the ice tonight.

"The Soviets pay their players to go out and play their best to glorify the USSR. They're not interested in selling anything. The consumer isn't important over there. There's no free enterprise." Ted drew powerfully on his cigarette once again and coughed, wiping brown spittle from his mouth and chin. "Their emphasis is on team play, not cultivating superstars who can sell crap like..." -- Ted glowered at his cigarette, threw it to the floor, and crushed it impassively under his heel -- "like cigarettes," he finished in a self-reproachful tone.

Ted shrugged, and continued to analyze. He sounded more like a professor than an electrical engineer. "So what's happening tonight is that the beer companies are making money

39

and we're losing the game. I feel like I've been had, that we've been had. We need a true miracle in the third period to pull this out."

Dennis looked confused. "D'you mean that because they don't have TV commercials in Russia, they're beating us tonight?"

"Exactly," Ted responded.

Dennis rubbed his chin thoughtfully. "You may have a point there," he acknowledged. "I'll have to think on it."

"Yes, you certainly should. Do just that," Ted enjoined. "The Soviet system has an edge tonight. Their team's been together for years and they're making us look pretty bad. Our guys've only been a team for a few days and they aren't clicking yet."

Dennis and I nodded somberly, and I silently vowed to abstain from chocolate bars for an entire week. I also vowed to give up sex equally as long which was an easy deprivation to swear to as I couldn't even recall when my last sexual experience had occurred.

Though the Canadians exerted themselves with all they had the remainder of the contest in pursuit of a come-from-behind victory, they were unable to avert national calamity. The final ignominious score read: USSR 7, Canada 3.

My thoughts? The Montreal Forum, I think, had been desecrated by a bunch of pinko atheists. They had dirtied the honor of a God-fearing country that **believes** in hockey, that **worships** hockey. They had dethroned Czar Nick way back in '17 and now, were they dethroning the Canadian hockey czars in '72, too? My stomach did a flip-flop at the very thought. The Soviet buggers! They had no respect, no respect at all!

The huge crowd streamed out of the Forum, chastened in defeat and speculating quietly among themselves as to what went wrong. Tears were cascading down Dennis' cheeks, and he was sniveling, "I lost a hundred dollars. I lost a hundred dollars. I shoulda bet on the Soviets!" The stunned atmosphere was akin to what you might find at the annual convention of the Daughters of the American Revolution were it to be announced that the genealogical credentials of the organization's president had been found fraudulent. The information is a true bombshell.

I didn't attend any more games, as they were played in other cities. Yet, I did follow the series in the media. By the time I left Québec, Team Canada had won only one of four games. The series had become a national disgrace. Some fed-up fans even booed the stars when they lost 5 to 3 in Vancouver -- which is on the order of the Daughters of the American Revolution jeering their own president at a national convention.

Every Canadian knows that individual talent did ultimately prevail over collective organization, that Team Canada did win the series, barely. It was a real cliffhanger (or should I say puckclinger?), going down to the final **seconds** of the eighth game, when a Canadian shot puckered the net somewhere in central Russia to bring home the sweetest victory ever. Team Canada had proved its superiority by persevering against incredibly long odds. They won, and along the way, they lost a certain smugness, their self-defeating hubris. The great Canadian national identity had been so traumatized that it would never be the same again.

On a Friday night, near the end of my sojourn in Montreal, I walked downtown to look for something to do. I stopped by the John Bull Pub to have a beer. I then found my way to the nearby Blue Bird Club, where I'd never been before. At the doorway I heard throbbing, potent live Country-Western music. The band was playing "I'm An Okie From Muskogee" and a packed house was dancing to it. My curiosity piqued, I paid admission and wriggled in.

I at last found a place to sit by asking a group of seven – four men, three women, all in their twenties, about my age – if I might occupy the empty chair at their table. They agreed, and I must confess it was not at all a bad place to join in. The three women, Monique, Angela, and Therese, were extremely good conversationalists. The four young men were burly, muscular ironworkers and the women were their friends. The seven of them were out on the town as a group. No one man seemed tied, at least publicly, to any one woman. The men took turns dancing with the women and I was invited to join the rotation.

I first danced with redhead Angela. Then I danced with blonde Therese to a few lively Country-Western numbers. Finally, I did a slower **pas de deux** with brunette Monique to a lanquidly-paced set that the band had launched into. Monique was a beautiful, buxom woman who enjoyed dancing close, a propinquity that was made more satisfying by the klutz who kept bumping into her backside, driving her forcefully against me. She too had been reading Pierre Vallieres' **Les Negres Blancs d'Amerique**. We discussed Vallieres' childhood of poverty in Montreal that had contributed to his revolutionary zeal for the Quebec Liberation Front and its demand for a free and independent Québec, a new nation inside Canada. For a dental hygienist Monique seemed unusually conversant with the world of ideas. When I asked her how she had happened to immerse herself in such an intellectual book, she replied simply, with a beguiling smile, "Because I am **Québecoise!**"

I regretted giving up Monique. Yet, I dared not seem possessive in front of the burly brutes who had brought her. I towered over them, yet they outnumbered me. So I had no choice but to follow the protocol we had established.

I began again with Angela, then to Therese, and, at long last, I rotated back to Monique. I certainly felt I had earned a return to her arms. And was it worth it! She was an excellent dancer as well as witty and charming. She also had, as far as I could discreetly estimate, forty-four inches worth of mammaries stuffed into a DD brassiere. I regarded her as a female metaphor for Mount Royal, as far as size went, but she was much more. She eclipsed the mountain in that she moved with a brilliant, fluid rhythm and grace that reflected the sunlight of Québec's best poetry and song. In short, I sort of liked her.

Suddenly, something happened that dramatically changed the evening. I heard unnatural voices from upstairs, voices out of place in a club. There was an anxiety in them that got through the music. Soon I smelt smoke and felt bodies surging against Monique and me on the dance floor. Screams followed, lots of them, and smoke began to fill the place, causing us to cough, irritating our eyes, and sharply reducing visibility. Everyone began to move toward the exit. Panic erupted in the chaos, and there was a growing and imminent danger of getting knocked down by the swelling human tide.

The force of the throng separated Monique from me. Bar patrons, trapped on the second floor, were jumping onto cars in the street. Some missed the relatively soft landing of a car top and hit pavement, seriously injuring themselves. The Blue Bird Club filled with thick, gray smoke that the strobe lights on the bandstand suffused eerily with a spectrum of green, orange, yellow, blue, and white light. I imagined that I had been consigned to a particularly punishing level of Dante's Hell. I reached for Monique, but only succeeded in getting my hand swacked and bloodied by a hard object, probably a beer bottle.

Panic pulsed like high-voltage electricity through the crowd. I thrust my massive frame ahead, forcing my 270 pounds against a bottleneck of people just ahead of me. I popped them free of the main mass of the throng and continued in their wake, much as a floating log is carried along in a river after a large logjam has been broken up.

Amazingly, like a miracle to me, I found myself just outside the Blue Bird Club, expelled by the cumulative force of the panicked crowd behind me. They had broken me loose and free much as I had unjammed a small knot of bar patrons ahead of me. The amorphous, anonymous surge behind cleared me well beyond the entrance to the club, where I looked up to see flames shooting twenty to thirty feet skyward through the Blue Bird roof. Ash and glowing ember spewed over a wide area. Smoke was billowing up in mammoth clouds.

As firefighters streamed water onto the inferno, monstrous clouds of steam roiled up and mixed with the smoke, blotting the sky completely from view. The flickering dome lights of police cars and firefighting vehicles reflected preternaturally off the ghastly base of the low-lying clouds of smoke and steam. It all struck me as a hellish blend of Kafka, Dante, and either wanton negligence or homicidal arson.

Quite a number had been injured, that was soon clear. People suffering from burns, cuts, scrapes, smoke inhalation, broken bones, bruises, and sprains were keeping ambulances and medics very busy. I counted thirty-seven victims lowered onto gurneys and rolled into ambulances that screamed away into the confused blackness of the night.

As I walked home -- it must've been two a.m. -- a thickset, balding man looked quizzically at me for no reason at all. Strange! But, after I arrived home and stood before a mirror, I could see the object of his puzzlement. It was my face, which flying ash and enveloping smoke had streaked black and gray.

I took a shower and tried to sleep, but I couldn't. Then I tried to read, yet concentration eluded me as fully as sleep had. The enormity of what had happened at the Blue Bird Club was beginning to sink in. I became highly nervous. I paced the halls on my floor and every other floor. I ate everything I could lay my hands on and drank several soft drinks from the lobby beverage dispenser.

Finally, about six a.m., I went out to see if I could find a morning newspaper. I did, from a vending rack on Pine Avenue, and I wish I hadn't. Thirty-six had died in the Blue Bird Club fire and fifty-four injured were in the hospital. The fire had been Montreal's worst since 1927 when seventy-seven children had perished in a conflagration at the Laurier Palace Theatre.

In coming days, pictures of the thirty-six dead were published. Among them were Monique, Angela, and Therese. The day I saw those pictures, I promised myself I would never get married. I have kept that promise.

44

Chapter 2

University of British Columbia, 1973

I almost didn't make it to Canada the summer of 1973. I applied to several universities but without success. So, I eventually gave up on the idea, and made plans to spend my summer at my alma matter, the University of California at Berkeley, writing and doing research, and visiting my parents in nearby Oroville. The semester had ended at Illinois State and I had even begun to pack my car, in early June, when I received a phone call.

"Is this Dr. G. Louis Heath?" the gravelly voice asked.

"Yes," I replied.

"Good morning to you! This is Charles Brauner at the University of British Columbia. Do you recall that you applied for a summer job here a few months ago?"

"Yes I do. I received a letter saying there was nothing available."

"Yes you did. That was my letter. But now we have an opening. We've had a heavier-than-expected enrollment in Sociology of Education and we now need to open a third section. I know it is very late to ask, but would you by chance be available to teach a third section for us?"

I told Brauner I was free, willing to take the job, and that $1,800 was fine for six weeks, plus round-trip mileage. We worked out an arrangement whereby my contract would be sent to "General Delivery" at the post office in Bozeman, Montana. There I would pick up the contract, sign it, and mail it back to the University on my way to Vancouver.

"When are you leaving?" Brauner asked.

"Tomorrow," I replied. "My car is packed and I'm ready to roll. You just changed my summer plans."

We talked a little more. I told Brauner I had read his philosophy of education book, and he said he'd seen reviews of some of my books, though he hadn't read any. I concluded the conversation by thanking Professor Brauner for the opportunity to teach at British Columbia. "You have a very fine faculty there," I said.

I had known Charles Brauner prior to his phone call only through his book, **Philosophy of Education** (New York: Ronald Press, 1962). He, then at Purdue, and Professor Robert W. Burns of Syracuse University, compiled the volume, a collection of articles by leading educational philosophers such as John Dewey, Harry S. Broudy, and Van Cleve Morris. Brauner had written a lengthy preface to give the student a helpful overview and point out specific things in each article to look for. Before I arrived at Illinois State in 1969, the Education Department had purchased 300 copies of the book and put them on the shelves of the University book-rental service. For several years, all the students in Philosophy of Education 231, a required class, studied Brauner and Burns, each borrowing a copy from the rental service for a small service charge. The sizable hardcover, a royal blue book with gold lettering, could usually be seen on campus without too much searching, carried under arms and lying on tables in the student union. The loan copies became tattered and broken over the years and they were retired from use shortly after I arrived. They have been replaced by texts and trade books that each professor now selects himself and which the students purchase in bookstores near campus.

I took my time getting to British Columbia, spending two weeks in Montana, and a week in Seattle, where I began to suffer terribly from an allergy, or something. My eyes cried with teary abandon interminably and my sinuses ran as though from behind floodgates which had been thrown open. I speculated that the cause was a plant or tree I wasn't used to.

Unfortunately, this problem was to bother me in the most excruciating fashion throughout my summer in Vancouver, where no doctor, of three I tried, was able to pinpoint the problem. The various medications they prescribed substantially relieved the symptoms for short periods of time, but they never made me well. It was not until I finally left Vancouver in August, and arrived in Kamloops, B.C., that the sickness began to fade. By the time I reached Saskatchewan, I was a well man.

I arrived at the University of British Columbia feeling miserable. On the short drive from Seattle to Vancouver, my tears blurred my view of the highway. I used up an entire box of kleenex, blowing my nose and wiping my eyes. In addition to my allergy, or whatever it was, by then I also suffered from something else, likely a virus, that made my entire body ache. What I wanted to do most was check into my residence hall, eat a meal, and go to bed.

In the residence-hall lobby, others looked sympathetically at me as I blew my nose and wiped my eyes continuously. I knew I had a face that had turned putty-white in Seattle, that I looked miserable.

After I picked up my key for room 214 in MacKenzie House (rent, $230 for the six-week summer session), I lugged my luggage up to my room. After taking more medicine and stuffing my pockets with kleenex, I drove to the edge of campus, near War Memorial Gymnasium, where I found a small Chinese restaurant. Famished, I ate voraciously, sneezing wildly and sweating profusely, and, of course, drawing more sympathetic stares.

Under the pitying gaze of the Chinese proprietor, I paid my bill, and went next door to a convenience store, where I bought some colas, apples, and sandwiches. Then I struggled back to my residence-hall room where I immediately konked out in a long, fitful sleep. I dreamed of the events that might follow for me in the wake of my grave sickness. Would I be able to teach? Could I physically make my presence felt at all, to impress on the Faculty of Education that I was on campus, trying to do my job, albeit very sick? I dreamed that I became a huge mountain of mucus, bigger than Grouse Mountain overlooking Vancouver, and that the viscid mass had begun to move. It accreted students,

47

buildings, rocks, and trees, and it picked up speed and engulfed the Faculty of Education Building with a slurping, gurgling sound, carrying it far off campus and depositing it on a beach, from where the whole revolting shebang washed out to sea!

The campus was located on a peninsula, Point Grey, that branched off from the land on which the city stood. Jutting majestically into the Strait of Georgia, it featured many fir trees, mostly on the fringes of the campus, that gave me a venerable sense of being in an ancient forest.

Since most the students in the Place Vanier residence hall complex were ardently talking about the Watergate hearings that many were watching on TV, I decided to include a short discussion of Watergate as part of my first day's educational offering. I wanted to talk about the wrongdoing as well as what might be wrong with the education of the officials involved and the values they espoused. Was Watergate an aberration or had the participants simply been unlucky enough to have been caught? The Watergate principals were all college graduates. Did they learn any of their dirty tricks in college, in fraternities, by cheating on exams, or what? Was there any relationship at all? These were all legitimate questions for my course, part of the syllabus of which was devoted to "politics and education."

I was still very sick Monday, the first day of summer session, but, by taking some over-the-counter medications, I felt a little better just before class at one p.m. Armed with a box of kleenex, I walked toward the Faculty of Education Building. I stopped every few steps along the way to blow my nose and wipe my eyes. It's going to be a helluva summer, I thought.

My first break of the summer came when I walked into my basement-level classroom. There were few students, only eighteen. That was certainly a plus. The fewer students I had, the better the chance I had of making it successfully through the six-week summer session. Eighteen struck me as a vast improvement on the enrollments of 75 and 79 in the other two sections of Education 470, Sociology of Education. They were taught by visiting professors from the University of Massachusetts (Dr. Emma Cappelluzzo) and Stanford University (a young assistant professor whom I never met). They worked too hard all summer, doubtless casting an envious eye on my small enrollment. With those kinds of numbers, for the salary paid (a pittance for the assistant professor from Stanford, who earned only $1,200), I could understand why the regular faculty at B.C. often didn't teach summers. Instead, the university hires faculty from other universities who want to travel to Vancouver.

Before discussing Watergate, I spent a few minutes on introductions, of myself and the students. Only four students were from Vancouver. The others were from the interior, the northern coast, and Vancouver Island. They hailed from such towns as Kamloops, Nelson, Dawson Creek, Prince George, Prince Rupert, Campbell River, Port Alberni, and Kelowna. All were teachers. They taught a broad range of subjects, mostly in high school. Eight were provisionally certified vocational education teachers who were taking my course to move a step closer to full accreditation. One had immigrated from New South Wales, Australia ("a bloody backward educational bureaucracy there") aboard "The Teacher Ship," a passenger ship chartered by the B.C. government to bring teachers to Canada during a time of great teacher shortage.

I informed the class that the texts for the class were my **The New Teacher: Changing Patterns Of Authority And Responsibility In The American Schools**, published by Harper and Row for $2.95 in paperback in the States, but priced at $3.95 in British Columbia, and my **Red, Brown, and Black Demands for Better Education**, by Westminster Press, listed at $3.95 in the U.S. but costing a dollar more in the University bookstore.

In an hour's lecture, I sketched what the six-week class covered. "As soon as I get an office and find out how things operate around here, I'll get a syllabus to you," I finished.

49

I then tried to get a discussion going on Watergate. "Who's been watching the Watergate hearings in here?" Everyone raised their hand. "Good," I smiled. "I'd like to talk about the hearings." I paused portentously, clearing my throat as if about to utter profound words. I sneezed violently and had to grab my box of kleenex from the desk and ply several tissues over my face for a full minute before I could resume. Blinking at the class through rheumy eyes to bring them back into focus, I discovered that I had forgotten what I had started to talk about. "Where was I?" I asked stertorously.

"Watergate!" said George loudly. "You were just beginning Watergate." George Iwasaki was a young, long-haired Japanese-Canadian clad in an army fatigue jacket, jeans, workshirt, and sandals, an outfit evoking the styles of three worlds – military, proletarian, and hippie.

"Thanks," I said. "That's what I was on, alright." This time I didn't pause portentously to clear my throat. It was proving too dangerous to my health. I went straight to the topic. "I want to discuss the relationship, if any, between the Watergate scandal and the American educational system. How could all those people in the Nixon Administration have gone to college and still be the kind of people who would engage in corruption and crime?"

George shot his hand up. "The American schools made Watergate possible because they teach corruption as a good way to get ahead, as long as you don't get caught. The Canadian schools teach the same stuff."

A sour expression appeared in the first row. It belonged to Archie Widener who taught in Kamloops. "George, I don't agree," he said emphatically, "with what you said about Watergate. I don't believe these people -- Haldeman, Mitchell, Magruder, Hunt, Dean, Ehrlichman, and the rest, those who've been criminal or corrupt or at least unprofessional -- I don't believe they've been taught to be bad by the schools. I think they are a deviation from what society and the schools teach. The bloody Watergate burglars just happened to take a crooked turn.

It's more their personal background and development than anything else." Archie scowled at George. "If you accept the view of the gentleman to my left here, then you would have to say that all political leaders are corrupt. I don't buy that at all. I think he's bloody off base."

Our chaotic discussion went on an hour, drawing in several participants. I would say that the time spent did not at all produce high-quality educational results, though it did help the nineteen of us to break the ice and it assisted greatly in getting me through the first two-hour class, during which I blew my nose at least once every three minutes and brushed tears from my eyes constantly. I was one hellacious piece of a Midwestern import of an excuse for a teacher!

In my class we had four of what we called "ferry people." Those were the four who had to catch the ferry for the trip across the Strait of Georgia to Vancouver Island every Friday afternoon. The reason their weekly ferry ride gave them an identity in my class is that in order to make the 3:15 ferry, they had to leave class fifteen minutes early. They argued that in the Vancouver traffic, they needed the extra quarter-hour to make sure they arrived at the terminal on time. When I countered that there was a 4:30 ferry, they pointed out that sometimes that ferry filled up before they could drive aboard if they were too far back in line. Gordon reinforced this argument with the sentimental pitch: "If we have to wait an hour for the 5:25, then we miss Friday supper with our families. Now wouldn't that be a shame after we've lived all week like prisoners in dormitory cells, eh?"

After weighing the arguments and conferring privately with others who knew the ferry schedule -- to be sure I wasn't being conned -- I established a policy that the "ferry people" could leave at 2:35 on Friday afternoons.

Ferry commuter Gordon and I became acquainted over several meals in the Place Vanier cafeteria. He loved to talk about his farm on Vancouver Island, halfway between Nanaimo and Victoria. He enthused, "You can't appreciate what real food is until you've had milk from our cow, vegetables from our garden, pork from our pigs, and mutton from our sheep." Gordon split his pepper-and-salt beard with a wide smile at the thought of the food produced on his farm. Then he frowned and poked a fork at his plate of cafeteria food. "This stuff is bloody terrible. It has so many additives that it makes me feel bad."

A native of Vancouver Island, Gordon was a friendly, independent-minded fellow, an industrial arts teacher in a rural school. He had left his occupation as a welder to teach on a provisional certificate, which stipulated he take summer courses to move toward full certification, something he did most happily. "In school, it's difficult to have an industrial accident, lose a finger or arm or burn yourself," he noted with his characteristic, broad smile. "And I get a lot of school holidays to spend on my farm."

One Monday, Gordon brought his twelve-year-old son Cy – short for "Cyrus" – to campus to spend the week with him, "so he can see the university and what goes on here." That was the Monday Gordon invited me for a weekend on his farm. "My wife and I talked it over this weekend," he smiled. "We'd love to have you as our guest next weekend."

I had to decline the invitation on account of my health problems. Often, in walking from Place Vanier to class, in spite of medication, my eyes would become so teary I could only find my way by constantly wiping them with kleenex. Several times in class, I found myself so congested that lecturing became a terrible ordeal, like speaking with a mattress stuffed down my throat and a pillow jammed into each nostril.

Standing before the class, pulling out one kleenex after another from the box I always carried with me, I attempted to convey enough information and ideas to justify my $1,800 salary and $200 travel allowance. I never fully achieved my goal. What I did achieve daily was to struggle through the first hour to the ten-minute break, and from there, through another painful hour to the end of class. What learning I may have caused was strictly a sidebar to my surviving two hellish hours each day. The motto of Illinois State University, which produces thousands of excellent new teachers each year, is "And gladly do we learn, and gladly do we teach." In British Columbia, the motto did not apply to me. There was nothing "gladly" about my ordeal.

And horror of horrors, the congestion and tears proved small misery compared to the rash that spread over my chest and back. The painful stinging and itching assailed me the entire six weeks and prevented me from sleeping normally. It was far worse than the worst case of poison oak I had ever contracted in California fighting fires four summers for the California Division of Forestry. I usually slipped into a light sleep about two a.m., from sheer exhaustion, but about four a.m. the needling discomfort would awaken me. I'd rise and go get some ice cubes from the refrigerator in the hallway alcove. Then I'd take a cold shower and rub the cubes over my back and chest. If that mitigation of the pain failed to enable me to sleep, at least it reduced the swelling and made me less miserable for a few hours. Usually it made it possible for me to have a decent interval of sleep.

Perhaps the happiest day in my life will be, I often thought, the day when I leave Point Grey. This is hell! But I also resolved to make the best of it, to see and learn as much as I could and meet some interesting people even though it had to be through a tremendous exertion of will. At times, literally, I thought I might die.

Yet thoughts of death did have counterpoints on the British Columbia campus. There were also thoughts, and visions, of life, some of them quite naked, for the University of British Columbia is the only campus I'm aware of that has its own nude beach. Called "Wreck Beach," it lies on the tip of the westward-jutting peninsula the campus sits on, on the northern side. It is a rocky beach, with some good stretches of sand, and the water is quite shallow for some distance out. But the bottom is excruciatingly sharp-rocky. It is a place where a good number of boats have crashed in storms into a premature death on the rocks.

From Place Vanier, all I needed to do was walk a hundred yards, crossing Northwest Marine Drive, and begin walking a steep path down the crags that stretch like a wall around much of the campus. Thus, though Wreck Beach can sort of said to be on campus, especially as viewed from the air, it is far less so than that bird's-eye perspective would suggest. In fact, the steep descent over and around rock outcroppings and through dense fir and chaparral, makes the place very difficult to reach. Wreck Beach is an isolated beach, offering a great deal of privacy, which is doubtless why it went nude in the first place.

Frankly, I'm not keen on nude beaches. I think they're largely a waste, a magnet for the wrong kind of people, the jetsam and flotsam of society, the riffraff that would well be better off inside somewhere, like a mental hospital. In fact, during my many years in California, I never set foot on or cast an eye on Devil's Slide, Black's Beach, or any of the other **au naturel, alfresco** Californications. But there I was in Canada, on a campus with a fabled beach, the famous "Wreck Beach." The question for me became very touristy: What could I say to the people back in Illinois when they asked, "Did you see the beach they have out there?"

So, one afternoon, I snuck, walking stealthily in a circumcuitous route, across Marine Drive, to the point near the road where I began my descent. And I must say the trip wasn't nearly as bad as I had feared. The path I took was well traveled, and I negotiated it rather easily, despite my illness, by taking my time, and holding on to an occasional bush or spindly tree. In fact, I felt a strong sense of accomplishment about the hike down once I reached the huge boulders overlooking the western flank of where the nude sunbathing and the skinnydipping began.

It was a perfect, calm, cobalt-blue day, hardly a break in the water as I arrived, some time between tides. A sweep of naked people, about a hundred in number, mostly women, stretched before me and around the bend. I still felt very ill, but maybe not so ill. I breathed in deeply the ocean breeze and felt a bit rejuvenated. Looking at a lot of life in the profound beauty of the human form, set against a gorgeous natural backdrop of water, sand, rock, and trees, lifted my spirit. I just knew, at that very moment, that I would make it through the summer and that I would get well.

The blind man who ran the basement cafeteria in the Faculty of Education Building was truly a marvel. Amazingly, he poured coffee with rapid precision. When I stared in disbelief at my still-extended cup after his quick pour, grateful that he had not scalded me, he said, "That's about all she'll hold, sir."

"How do you know it's full?"

"I can hear," he replied, "and I can feel how much I have poured."

I went to that small cafeteria daily, and I never saw him spill a drop of anything. He made no errors, and he operated a very efficient lunchroom. That beloved blind man literally knew his business like the palm of his hand.

One of my colleagues at McGill had been professor emeritus F. Henry Johnson of the University of British Columbia. He had visited McGill to teach a five-week-long history of education course. Dr. Johnson, a tall, thin, silver-haired, soft-spoken gentleman was also an excellent scholar, author of **A Brief History of Canadian Education** (Toronto: Macmillan of Canada, 1968), and numerous scholarly articles. Professor John Lipkin told me at McGill, "Henry's the kind of fellow who you can always call on to deliver a paper at a convention. He's an active scholar, even though he's retired. He still teaches some."

At McGill, Henry had stayed at modern Molson Hall, a university student residence far up Mount Royal, above the Royal Victoria Hospital. Three or four times, I hiked up there, as steep a climb as Montreal offers on pavement, to have lunch with him at Bishop Mountain Hall, a roundhouse-shaped cafeteria serving four surrounding halls, including Molson. Usually we were joined by Stanton, a middle-aged teacher from a St. Louis, Missouri parochial high school, who was at McGill studying conversational German in "a German immersion program." We enjoyed leisurely lunches with lots of discussion ranging widely over many interesting topics such as the dockworkers strike against the port of Montreal, which had paralyzed shipping for weeks, and whether Québec might ever secede from Canada. Those were great lunches. I recall them fondly.

At the University of British Columbia, I ran into the retired F. Henry Johnson in the Faculty of Education building on one of his rare visits to campus. I told him that my sinuses, eyes, and skin were suffering terribly from something in the B.C. environment and that I had to take two kinds of pills, one green, one orange, three times daily, as prescribed by my doctors to keep the symptoms in modest check, and that, on account of the heavy medication, I slept ten to twelve hours a day, cumulatively, in small intervals of two and three hours, whenever exhaustion and the pills in tandem overtook the pain.

Henry speculated, "It might be cedar. A lot of people have an allergic reaction to that here. Sometimes when I chop cedar at my home for firewood, my hands break out in a rash for a while."

"Just great," I said. "Now all I have to do is cut down all the cedar trees in and around Vancouver!"

I talked regularly in the cafeteria with Brock, a professor of mathematics from Sydney, Australia. "I completed my Ph.D. here eight years ago," he noted. "Since then the salaries haven't gone up at all. And tenure is much harder to get in Canada than in Australia. We don't have to be on probationary status nearly as long as the Canadians."

Brock had arrived in Vancouver in late June from Oxford University, where he had spent the first part of a sabbatical that had begun in January. His wife and kids were to join him in September for five months in British Columbia, the final part of his sabbatical. "I couldn't afford to take them on the complete sabbatical with me," he remarked.

Meanwhile, in his wife's absence, Brock filled the need for female companionship by often dining and going to movies with June, a public health nurse from Hay River, in the Northwest Territories. She was on campus to attend summer classes related to her job. It was not romance, only middle-aged friendship between two people who had recently turned forty. June even helped Brock locate an apartment in anticipation of the arrival of his family and assisted him in shopping for furniture for it.

One of my most memorable students was also Australian. He was stocky, tanned Aldo Douglass, about thirty-five, who had an aquiline nose that contrasted sharply with otherwise heavy features and cashew-brown frizzy hair that clung thickly most of the way down the nape of his neck, giving him a curiously disheveled, though quite clean, rakish, earthy air. Aldo nearly always wore loud yellow Bermuda shorts, a bright purple, short-sleeved shirt, and down-at-heel soccer shoes so that he could go directly from class to the soccer pitch to compete in a summer-session league. He was a member of the all-star, all-Aussie team, comprised of other Australians who taught in small, interior B.C. towns and whom he saw only annually at the University of British Columbia summer session.

Aldo was a most articulate, intelligent fellow, with a good educational background, a lot of it owing to his own study. He was well-read. That was obvious to me from talking with him after class, during break, and in the Place Vanier cafeteria. He had the attitude of a good student. He took pride in the quality of his mind and strove to improve it incessantly, though formally, he had but two years of Australian teacher training. It was to advance toward his bachelor's degree that Douglass returned

57

summer after summer to Point Grey. Yet, intellectually, Aldo was far beyond a mere bachelor's degree.

Aldo had taught nine years in New South Wales before leaving the "totalitarian bureaucracy" there. According to his term paper, the Australian teacher is so "repressed" and so "subjugated" that many, beginning in 1965, leapt at the opportunity to take "the escape route to Canada." The emigration of Australian teachers to Canada reached a peak in 1968 when the Peninsula and Orient's ship **Canberra** -- dubbed "The Teacher Ship" -- sailed from Sydney to Vancouver in June with 450 Australian teachers aboard. "My salary in New South Wales after nine years of teaching, in 1968, was $216 per month clear (take home pay)...I regarded that salary as 'sweat shop' wages to people who were supposed to be 'professionals.' Whenever either the government or the administration started to appeal to our sense of professionalism, we knew that we were about to be, and I cannot think of a better term for it -- so pardon my vulgarity -- 'screwed.'"

Aldo had taught five years in frigid Dawson Creek, in British Columbia's sparsely populated northern interior. Like him, almost all the Australians had immigrated to teach in isolated communities where they inevitably clashed with the usual ways of doing things. "Many British Columbians still have remnants," he noted in his term paper, "of a traditional British reserve about their behaviour patterns, like being quiet in places marked 'QUIET.' Australians, on the other hand, are raucous, contemptuous, holy cow kickers with unpredictable behaviour patterns." He pointed out that the unusual and outrageous came to be accepted, and even expected, from himself and his countrymen. "Swinging from the rafters of the gymnasium at lunch time, singing modern songs loudly in school corridors during class time, eating a large, juicy apple whilst teaching a grade eight history class, shooting water pistols at students in the library area, are all accepted because it is done by the Australian...I do not feel that the students are laughing at me. I feel they laugh with me because I provide some comic relief and

I can assure you that one needs some comic relief in Dawson Creek, B.C. during the winter...It was very difficult for me to be appointed as a Department Head in a school...I was faced with a hostile staff because I was a foreigner and an Australian to boot. I do not think the hostility would have been so great had I been English because British Columbians still gravitate to the 'Old Country' syndrome. Once I had convinced my staff that I was not going to attempt a coup d'état and haul down the Maple Leaf from the flag pole and run up the Southern Cross in its stead, then could we commence the business of educating our charges. (I rushed home and learned the Canadian National Anthem thoroughly and on the rare occasions that it is sung in the school, I made sure that I sang the loudest and the sweetest.) I knew that I had been accepted when I was in the Staff Lounge at lunch time and the British Columbians came over to where I was sitting and sat and talked to me. I no longer had to go over and join them.

"Just when I thought that I had really adjusted to the way of life in British Columbia, I had the dubious honour of being asked to help select the School Cheerleading Squad. The idea of the school sex queens being asked to display themselves in a series of gyrations and hearing their inane ditties to help 'psych up' the home team was as alien to me as going to teach Mandarin to the Mongolians. I foolishly opened my big mouth to express my horror and I was drummed off the Staff Cheerleading Selection Committee. I was told that if I did not approve of the system, I should not have left Australia!"

Three other term papers were also noteworthy, as follow:

T. R. McDonald, "Social Considerations In High School Counselling," 33 pages. I gave McDonald a grade of A- for this paper. On the strength of his performance in my class, I wrote three references in support of his applications to master's degree programs at three American universities, including Washington State University. McDonald's paper presented several cases of problem students he had himself counseled, students who wanted

59

vocational and technical careers and whom the high school curriculum served poorly. For example, Manfred: "Manfred came to us in grade eight with an above average scholastic record. His father was a highly skilled motor mechanic and Manfred enjoyed a good home life with three younger brothers. He completed an average grade eight programme and as his school counsellor I spent some time with the boy and his parents discussing his future plans. Neither the boy nor his parents were interested in university education. The boy was extremely mechanically minded and had recently become interested in practical electronics. At this point it was decided he should follow the vocational programme and ultimately complete a suitable four year apprenticeship programme in a mechanical or electrical trade.

"During the summer holiday, I received a telephone call from the father asking if Manfred could be placed in the Academic Stream in grade nine the following September. When I asked why, I was told that their schoolteacher niece had advised them that the vocational programme was for failures and that they 'should go to the school and make a fuss about it.'

"Manfred entered the academic programme in grade nine the following September. At the end of the year he scraped a pass, but I began to hear more and more comments from teachers concerning his behaviour and lack of interest. He returned the following year to grade ten still in the Academic Stream. His year was a disaster right from the start. After many sessions with him, he revealed that he was constantly quarrelling with his parents in an attempt to return to the vocational programme he had first planned. The parents were equally adamant he was not going to be a 'failure.'"

After discussing three other Manfreds, some with far worse problems, the sapling-thin McDonald, who wore thick glasses beneath a dense thatch of always fastidiously combed, brilliantly brylcreemed hair, drew close. He concluded that the high schools should cease their myopic obsession with pre-university curricula and develop vocational and technical "streams" that are substantial and prestigious and which lead to an alternate style of success and good jobs. He hoped these "streams" would be equal to the challenge of developing the potential of the troubled Manfreds of British Columbia.

Charles Baldwin, "The U.S. Law School Admission Test And The Canadian Legal Profession," 27 pages. "...To enter law school in English Canada, Canadian students must score high on the **Law School Admission Test**, a test developed by the American aptitude testing company, Educational Testing Services (ETS), of Princeton, New Jersey...This is shameful!...Why must Canada rely on an American firm's tests to select its future lawyers?...What does this portend for the unique system of jurisprudence we have if we continue to depend on a test designed to select the law students for a different legal system?...How independent can we claim to be if the test scores mailed out by a U.S. testing firm to our Canadian law schools are allowed to remain the crucial variable in determining admission?..." Baldwin concluded, "We must, of course, develop our own law school admission test and stop this inane reliance on ETS. It is truly an obscene and degrading dependence..."

Baldwin had an especially ardent interest in his topic. Then a teacher in Nelson, B.C., he had recently been admitted to law school. He had, needless to say, become very upset at the process he had had to undergo to achieve that admission.

Charles Baldwin made me feel a surge of great pride when he told me, "The only reason I am taking this course this summer is out of sheer interest. I enrolled in it when I saw the list of books you had published in a **Vancouver Sun** article on you."

Colin T. Bowen, "Apartheid And Education In South Africa," 32 pages. I had become better acquainted with Colin than most the class. Colin and I had even made a couple visits to the faculty club together for drinks. The UBC faculty club was the only one in Canada I visited that featured chi-chi, miniskirted cocktail waitresses. I have no idea why. My one conjecture is that it had something to do with Wreck Beach. But beyond that I have no clue.

Colin had begun a paper on discrimination against non-white immigrants in Vancouver, including some very exploitative, sub-minimum wage hiring that summer. However, he had switched to South Africa when he discovered a treasure trove of materials on the topic in Sedgewick Library. The mustachioed, lean, glasses-wearing 25-year-old proved an excellent researcher as he synopsized and synthesized his sources well. He produced telling, incisive analyses and drew inferences from his data so well that he earned the third highest term paper grade in the class. "By 1968, the per-capita expenditure on black South African children was one-eighth the amount spent on white children...The UNESCO report on apartheid states that South African school books teach the black South African that he occupies an inferior position in society. White children are taught that Europeans are superior and that blacks are primitive and barbaric...

"Black parents must pay fees and bear the cost of textbooks in order for their children to attend secondary school, while, in stark contrast, such education is entirely free for white children...The black dropout rate is exceedingly high for economic reasons alone at the secondary level...Black enrollment in institutions of higher education is extremely small...Only 485 blacks in 1967 passed the university entrance examinations...

"And so, what is the future for South Africa?...It seems to me that there can be only two basic futures. One stretches out like a broad vista, a stark, crimson horizon, a wide-flung expanse of destitute, internecine land, the entirety of South Africa, smeared, daubed, and pooled with the blood of the Afrikaners, the whites, as well as with much, much black blood. Only the realization of the other future will prevent racial civil war. That future revolves around granting the black complete civil rights, all those the white enjoys, and opening up all levels of the educational system to develop the infinite resource of black potential, which up to now has been left almost completely undeveloped…"

Colin also presented some very specific recommendations in his paper, including, "We ought to boycott the imported South African canned goods, especially fruit, that now appear regularly on Vancouver grocery shelves."

Nigel Swift was a memorable student. A thickset, short, middle-aged biology teacher who wore glasses as thick as a Coke bottle, he sported a brushcut and carried himself in a ramrod, military-style posture. He told the class about one of his experiences teaching Indians in the B.C. interior. One day he had positioned his entire class at the microscopes in the school lab. "Now take the needles before you," he ordered, "and make a little prick in your finger. It won't hurt if you just prick lightly. You can't get infected because the needles are sterilized."

The 15-year-old students were to smear a drop of blood onto a slide for viewing.

Johnny Greenshirt, an Indian, refused. "I'm not going to stab myself!" he yelled and threw his needle at Nigel. "You do it to yourself! You're big and fat and have lots of blood!"

Nigel walked over to Johnny's lab table and bent over the young man, trying diplomatically to convince him to perform the task. "Everyone else is doing it the way it should be done, Johnny. It's part of the assignment, to see what **your own blood** looks like magnified a hundred, 250, and 500 times. You don't want to diagram someone else's bloody blood, eh? Don't you want to see the good Indian blood that pulses through your veins? Wouldn't that be great, eh?" asked Nigel, smiling and putting a friendly hand on the young man's shoulders.

Without warning, from where he sat on his stool, Johnny landed a vicious blow to Nigel's nose, vulnerably located but a couple feet away. The punch broke Nigel's nose and glasses.

Rivulets of blood flowed down his face. "Now I have my blood!" shouted Johnny. "You put your own blood on my slide, teacher!"

"I was as angry as I've ever been," recalled Nigel, "and I retaliated with my own blow that knocked Johnny off his stool and broke his nose, too. In fact, he lay unconscious on the floor a while, and I had to bring him to with a whiff of formaldehyde. As my head cleared and I got control of myself, I realized what a terrible thing had happened. I had hit a student! Teachers aren't supposed to clobber students...

"I knew he'd been having problems at home and that getting thrown out of school would be no help to him either. So, I quickly pulled Johnny to his feet and had a couple of the biggest kids in the class help me carry him down to the washroom and stationed them outside to keep others out while Johnny and I went in.

"Once we got inside, Johnny immediately took another punch at me, but I jumped out of range and grabbed him. 'Look here, Johnny!" I said. "We have to settle this thing peacefully, right now! Do you want to get thrown out of school for good, eh?' He shook his head and winced through his bloodied teeth. I could see the pain in his eyes. The front of his shirt was covered in blood, just like mine.

"I released my hold on his shirt and backed off. I said that I wanted to apologize and tried to smile, but couldn't because it hurt my broken nose so much. So I extended my hand and we shook. That was a big beginning for us.

"I couldn't smile, but I managed to explain my plan to Johnny. Neither of us would report the fight, and we'd say, when others brought it up that it had been no big deal, not a fight at all. Only a lab accident. We'd say that indeed we were good friends.

"I said that I would pay the doctor's bill for repairing Johnny's nose. He agreed to this by nodding. His nose was broken a lot worse than mine and he wasn't in any condition to talk, at least not right away. As I talked -- God it was painful to talk with that fractured nose -- Johnny and I used paper towels that we wet in the sink to clean the blood off ourselves. When we got finished in the washroom, we were far from friends, but we had our plan worked out, mutual self-interest you might say.

"And we stuck with that plan. We sort of grew with it, eh. And during the next two-and-one-half years, till he graduated, I went out of my way to help Johnny. And I'm happy to say he accepted my assistance and was nice in return. We got along real well after that fight. The strength of his character came to the fore. He had a lot of dignity, even though he came from a brawling, boozing home. I even gave him money regularly for clothes, food, and other essentials, because his family was on welfare and seemed determined to drink up anything they were supposed to spend on him...After he graduated from high school, I paid Johnny's way through trade school and he's a mechanic today...

"I think Johnny gave me the most personal and professional satisfaction of any one student over all my 26 years of teaching so far," concluded lifelong bachelor Nigel, aged 52. "Johnny even invited me to be the best man at his wedding. I thought that was my greatest reward ever!" enthused Nigel. "But there was an even greater reward to come. Johnny named his baby son Nigel in my honor!"

George Iwasaki, perhaps the most sensitive to the plight of minorities of anyone in the class, sat murmuring repeatedly, "Nigel Greenshirt...," as though processing the profound human story he had just heard, as if making the first name and surname, that did not seem to belong together, connect properly on his tongue. Selma Trollope in the middle row, to his right, was so moved that she was quietly crying, dabbing her eyes with her green-on-white embroidered ST handkerchief. And I was moved, too, deeply so.

Teachers are the target of a lot of criticism, much of it thoroughly undeserved. Occasionally a Nigel Swift appears among our humble ranks and does something that confers a great humanitarian cachet to a profession that must survive many of society's social problems before they can get on with their professional work. Nigel not only survived. He took the remains of a tragic confrontation and built on it a beautiful student-teacher relationship that saved both student and teacher and continued after Johnny graduated to a kind of fulfillment that is truly inspiring. He reconstructed that young man's life after they had given way to the violence within themselves. They conquered their craven hearts that had pumped venous blood onto their hands, faces, and shirts, and they built a future together.

Nigel is proof that someone must care on an intimate, personal level for the most troubled kids in order for them to build a successful life through our schools. Though initially galvanized by fear and self-interest, he soon transcended that, achieving what the Franciscan sisters who teach with me at Mount St. Clare College in Clinton, Iowa term "the joy of service." That joyous obedience and service through sacrifice for others is not only central to our mission statement. It was a big part of what made Nigel's efforts work for Johnny Greenshirt.

That summer, the Montreal Expos were in contention to win the National League Eastern Division title throughout July and August. As the only major league baseball team in Canada at the time, they compelled the attention of Canadians everywhere. They did more than any federal bilingual-bicultural program or law up to that time to unify Canada. They also fostered a certain degree of bilingualism in the Place Vanier residence halls' TV room. We learned the **joual** French equivalents of English baseball terms: **but** (base), **lanceur** (pitcher), **receveur** (catcher), **interieur** (infield), **arret-court** (shortstop), **balle jointure** (knuckle ball), **marbre** (home plate), and so on. The bilingualism the Expos games induced was contagious, and some in the TV room coined new terms. For example, the slang phrase "to Montreal" meant leaving the TV room for a bathroom visit and "un Bee Cee" was our Canadian French for a beer.

Bilingual dialogue could be regularly heard in the TV room. For example: "Ken Singleton got a single, and then he stole second **but**. After that, he stole the third baseman's **but**. Then Bob Bailey doubled him **marbre**, and Bailey stole the third baseman's ass. Then Steve Renko, the Expo's **lanceur**, came to the plate and bunted a **balle jointure** to the **interieur** and had his ass thrown out."

"Please give me un Bee Cee!"

The New Democratic Party held its annual, national, three-day convention in the University of British Columbia's War Memorial Gymnasium during my course. I sat in on the proceedings one afternoon, observing from one of the cantilevered spectators' galleries that span the length of each side of the gym. I listened to the national party leader, David Lewis, and British Columbia's New Democratic Party (NDP) Premier, Dave Barrett. They and others, at varying levels of shrillness, eloquence, and intellectual capacity, brought eye-opening scrutiny to bear upon the Canadian economy and society.

The flyer I picked up in the lobby seemed to echo what many of the speakers, representing every region of Canada, were saying. "Many corporations are not paying their fair tax," the flyer, printed on recycled paper, began. "For example, 556 of 681 oil and gas producers pay no tax at all. Shell Canada, one of our impoverished multinational subsidiaries, earned more than $516 million from 1964 to 1969, yet during that time, it paid not one cent of income tax, thanks to a vast network of tax concessions, depletion allowances, and other dodges. But the situation improved dramatically in 1970! That year, Shell finally got around to paying some tax. It paid $16 million on net earnings of $123 million, a rate of 13 percent. That is about half the rate paid by most people earning no more than nine or ten thousand dollars a year. These low-income people don't benefit from tax breaks and chartered accountants. All they have are bills!"

The flyer continued by giving a rundown on Canadian "corporate bums" who paid absolutely no tax. The following statistics surprised even cynical me: 54 of 105 pulp and paper mills paid no tax; 31 of 36 iron mines paid no tax; 8 of 27 distilleries paid no tax; 77 of 215 motor vehicle and motor vehicle parts manufacturers paid no tax; 15 of 22 major appliance companies paid no tax; and 36 of 141 pharmaceutical manufacturers paid no tax. Total estimated unpaid tax: $3.3 billion!"

The flyer concluded, "It is obvious free enterprise in Canada is walking on crutches. If you are feeling a tremendous, financial burden these days, it is because you and your taxes are the crutches...What must be done?...Abolish special concessions for corporations so that all of them pay their fair tax. The corporate welfare bums must shoulder their proper responsibility in the economy and should not be allowed to get rich abusing the working man!"

Young Dave Barrett, then 42, the New Democratic Party Premier of B.C., was a hard-working, very competent leader, well-educated, with a master's degree from St. Louis University in Missouri. He had a penchant for the flamboyant and comic. He made such comments, reported in the press, as "On a warm day I have an IQ of 105." At a rodeo that summer, after he had thrown a dried bullchip further than any other contestant, he proclaimed himself "the champion bullchip thrower."

I had an opportunity to talk with Barrett after I insinuated myself into a small huddle of reporters who had gathered about him, like flies to a bullchip. I asked questions right along with the media people. The premier really opened up to us. "I'm going to get rid of tax concessions for all business and industry before the year's out," he proclaimed, "especially for the Americans...I'm also going to raise the price of natural gas we export to the U.S. by almost 90 percent...My social legislation will also be going into high gear, especially Mincome. Everyone over 60 will get a minimum of $209 a month and there'll be free medicine for those over 65...I've already gotten rid of the previous government's, Social Credit's, labor laws that made it possible to impose compulsory settlements on decent, hard-working people who are trying their best to do a good job and make ends meet...And I'm going to see to it that taxes on privately-held mineral rights will go from $100,000 a year that we're getting now to at least $25 million in the very near future."

In his brief, impromptu news conference with the press, Barrett came across surpassingly well, the genuine populist who displayed great concern for people. The image of himself that he dramatized in War Memorial Gymnasium was far from comic. He demonstrated a tremendous grasp of the issues in a very articulate way. I was impressed.

As we broke up, Barrett talked individually with everyone briefly. "I'm not a reporter," I told him in a sheepish voice, "just a visiting American lecturer for the summer." Barrett's eyes went wide and he seemed tentative throughout a painfully long silence. Finally, the tentativeness in his eyes gave way to an agate hardness. He briskly wheeled on his heel so that I got a full, close-up view of his backside as he stormed out of the gym.

I stood alone in the center of the raw emptiness of the huge pavilion-style structure, a fingered fist projecting toward the immense rafters.

Dr. John Bremmer, the B.C. Commissioner of Education, gave a Thursday afternoon tea in mid-July for the University community. It was held in the Faculty of Education building in the first-floor lounge, directly behind the spacious, glossy marble foyer that I found so appealing every time I entered. Often such teas draw an embarrassing few, sometimes no one, even though the person giving it may be an important personage. So a gimmick was tried: locating the canapés, petits fours, and a samovar of tea in plain eye-catching view of the students as they entered the province's citadel of pedagogy. This allowed the redolence of sweets to invade their sugar-addicted Canadian nostrils. It was like giving an addict a whiff of his mojo.

The strategy worked well. The students came in droves, many not caring or even knowing, ever, before or after, that Dr. John Bremmer, British Columbia's top educator, stood to one side of the table from which they grabbed the goodies that had precipitated their voracious stampede into the lounge.

I had encouraged my students to avail themselves of the opportunity to sparkle with their educational leader. "It's an opportunity you'll likely not have again," I said. "You, as teachers, would do well to meet him. Maybe you'll learn something, and at least you can say you shook the commissioner's hand and talked with him." Thus inspired, most my students joined the stampede over the marble onto the thick lounge carpet, toward the refreshments. I thought it all a very nice accent to summer school.

Bremmer was a middle-aged Briton who had established a reputation by launching an innovative educational program in Philadelphia called "The School Without Walls," about which he'd written a book by the same title, that I had read. Learners were free in Bremmer's program to go out on their own and visit museums, historical sites, and such.

I learned after leaving B.C. that Dr. Bremmer became the first North American educator to be fired via TV. Premier Dave Barrett, with all the off-the-wall panache he could muster, announced on the evening news that "Dr. Bremmer has been a flop as Commissioner of Education and he will be fired."

Dr. Bremmer responded by suing the province for breach of contract. He won $30,000 in severance pay.

The average price I paid for gas throughout the summer was 55.6 cents per Canadian-sized gallon. I paid $2.98 for five gallons at Earl's Service Centre in Moosomin, Saskatchewan; $3.61 for 6.7 gallons at Charlton's Village Service Centre at 2190 Western Parkway, Vancouver; $2.25 for four gallons at the

Last Chance Mohawk, R.R. 2, Hope, B.C. (The attendant spoke with a thick German accent and claimed to be Adolf Hitler's grandson.); $3.85 for 6.6 gallons at Brooks Shell Service, Brooks, Alberta; and, many more, equally exciting service stops, to arrive at my average. The spot where I bought gas most often was the one closest to campus, the Home Oil Station at 10th and Sasamat ("Your Home Service Centre On Point Grey") where regular was priced at 53.8 cents a gallon.

The rent for all the fleabag motels and hotels I stayed at driving to and from B.C. averaged $8.22. Room 9 at the Leggatt Hotel in Billings, Montana went for $5. Room 16 in the Leland Hotel at 301 Victoria Street in Kamloops, B.C. set me back $8.40. Number 29 at the Montcalm Gordon Motor Hotel at 2280 Pembina Highway in Fort Garry, Manitoba, cost $10.50. The Beaubier Gordon Hotel in Brandon, Manitoba charged me $4.73 for a simple, clean room. And, the lowest-priced of all was the ancient yet solid Imperial Hotel in Swift Current, Saskatchewan, where the old clerk gave me reliable #310 for the going rate of $3. ("Put a towel over the rip in the shade and the neon lights won't come through so bad," he advised.)

I became engrossed in four books during my short tenure on Point Grey. Only one was popularly written, which anyone might enjoy, and that was Eric Nicol's **Vancouver** (Toronto: Doubleday, 1970). The book offered a good capsule history of the city and a compelling survey of what it offered the visitor. The author was a well-known columnist for the **Vancouver Province**. The second book was John Rodgers' **Birds of Vancouver** (Bryant Publications, 1971, $3.50). This supplemental handbook to the standard field guides helped me to identify several birds that I saw for the first time. I shall never forget the thrill of sighting my first Black Oystercatcher and Hudsonian Godwit on English Bay.

The third and fourth books were specialized, the province only of the educational historian. They were James Sandison's

Schools of Old Vancouver (Vancouver Historical Society, 1971, $4.00) and Kenneth Waites' **The First Fifty Years, Vancouver High Schools, 1890-1940**, published in 1943 and now out of print. I purchased the 1971 book at Duthie's Bookstore on Robson Street in downtown Vancouver, just east of the main public library, where I borrowed the 1943 volume by depositing $20 until I returned it. Both books were exceedingly well researched and, I believe, well enough written to engage any reader who had anything approaching an interest in the subject matter.

Many Americans, and maybe even a few Canadians, are unaware of the Canadian role in the Vietnam War. A small force of Canadian troops served nineteen years in Vietnam, first as a member of the International Control Commission, and later with the International Commission of Control and Supervision. They participated in the ICCS to police a cease-fire but instead had spent much of their time observing a war.

Unfortunately, the Communists tended to view the Canadian observers as pro-American. The Viet Cong even went so far as to capture two Canadian officers, Captain Ian Patten of Ottawa and Captain Fletcher Thomson of Etobicoke, Ontario, on June 28th, just before my Soche of Ed class began at British Columbia. The VC had suspected the two of assisting South Vietnamese troops in a recent attack.

Two weeks later External Affairs Minister Mitchell Sharp announced Canada would withdraw her 289-man force on July 31st. The Viet Cong immediately released Thomson and Patten. Apparently the capture of the two officers had been the final straw for a Canadian government which had clearly seen the handwriting on the wall --**WITHDRAW!** -- a graffito my government would not heed till April 30, 1975, the official date of U.S. withdrawal.

I followed the news on Vietnam very closely that summer because my main writing project then dwelt on American opposition to the war. The 2,800-page manuscript, which I slaved over in B.C. though very ill, was published in 1976 as the 636-page **Mutiny Does Not Happen Lightly,** with a preface by Senator Ernest Gruening, one of only two Senators -- the other was Wayne Morse -- to vote against the Gulf of Tonkin Resolution that launched the U.S. into that tragic Asian war.

The Canadian troops flew home, stopping first in Vancouver. I viewed TV coverage of their arrival on the nightly news report, "The National." The soldiers emerged briskly from their plane, appearing relieved to set foot on Canadian soil. They enthusiastically waved their berets at the crowd and smiled toothily. I was elated for them. "Thank you Canada, for leading the way back to international sanity!" I shouted as I watched the news, drawing both curious stares and approving smiles in the Place Vanier TV room.

Maybe my government would decide to face up to the inevitable, too, and withdraw, I thought. The purposeless fighting in Southeast Asia had gone on so very, very long, wasting thousands of young lives, much moral capital, and billions of dollars that could have gone toward higher, humanitarian purposes.

The summer of 1973 had its share of labor-management strife. A rotating strike by Air Canada ground employees went on throughout my course, affecting 35 airports and causing numerous flight cancellations. Pulp and paper workers struck, too, and most disruptive of all, there was a national railway strike.

By the time I departed for home in August, the national rail strike by craft workers, engineers, conductors, and brakemen, had precipitated so much economic disarray that Prime Minister Trudeau had had to call a special session of Parliament. I followed that session on TV and in newspapers as I drove the Trans-Canada for four days.

I stayed my first night out in a creaky, downtown Kamloops, B.C. hotel where I watched about 200 striking railway workers on TV picket members of Parliament as they arrived on the Hill for the emergency session. The picketers carried a variety of signs; for example, "Local 1127 On Strike," "C.P. Rail Is Not Fair To Labor," and "En Greve, C.P. Rail." Unwilling to remain peaceful picketers, a mob of them rampaged past RCMP guards and forced their way into the Parliament Building, smashing windows as they surged through corridors.

When I reached Saskatchewan two days later, a wage settlement had been reached with most the railroad workers. I stayed my third night out at the venerable, though deteriorating (yet still solid) Imperial Hotel in Swift Current, near the railway switchyard, where a good number of away-from-home "rails" roomed. They were part of a small group that had yet to become a party to the national settlement.

Entering the lobby, I passed two men leaving the hotel carrying picket signs. Ahead, amid a clutter of picket signs, ranged about an old Motorola TV that belonged in a museum, several "rails" were taking a break from the picket line. I briefly took a seat among them to watch the news and talk. One of them volunteered the information that the entire group rooming in the Imperial belonged to the Canadian Brotherhood of Railway, Transport, and General Workers, a renegade union that was still doggedly holding out.

All this felt very familiar and comfortable to me, the son of a man who worked 35 years as a conductor and brakeman for California's Western Pacific Railroad. It also felt very good.

Chapter 3

Dalhousie University, 1974

I applied everywhere in Canada I had not taught, but I failed to land a job for the summer of 1974. Lakehead University talked as though it planned to offer me a position, but at the last moment dashed my hopes that they had raised so high. I was sorely disappointed, yet I decided to travel north again anyway, to Halifax, to see what Nova Scotia was like and work on a project I had begun several years before. I stayed in a room in Howe Hall, number 366 Bronson House, at Dalhousie University and labored on the final chapters of my book on the American radical group, the Students for a Democratic Society, which appeared in 1976 as the 528-page **Vandals In The Bomb Factory**. When I wasn't writing, which was a decent amount of the time, I was occupied with the events and people I describe in this chapter.

Next door to me lived a talkative, friendly, black ex-convict, thirty-year-old Rascoe, who had grown up on the poor side of Halifax, in Africville, near the Bedford Basin. Rascoe was out on parole from Dorchester Penitentiary, where he had served four years for auto theft. (He had hot-wired a Toyota and a day later was apprehended with it on the ferry plying the Bay of Fundy between Digby, Nova Scotia and St. John, New Brunswick.) He had recently found a job as a department store stockroom clerk and was staying the summer at "Dal," as the University is popularly known (because a room is relatively inexpensive there and it is located in residential Halifax, an easy walk from the downtown business district), at least until he could save enough money to rent an apartment.

Owing much to the fact that we lived in adjacent rooms, Rascoe and I often talked and soon we became rather chummy.

Regularly we walked down the hill Dal stood upon for a meal or snack together, usually at Diana Sweets Restaurant on Spring Garden Road, a couple blocks below campus. We liked Diana's because it offered good food and an appealing, homey atmosphere accented by a very obese Bassett hound that waddled from table to table begging morsels of food with a languid series of woofs, accompanied by the most forlorn eyes I had ever seen in a Bassett. "Old Blue" was his name, short for "Old Bluenose." Originally, he'd been "Bluenose," namesake of the famous racing clipper "Bluenose," built in Lunenburg, Nova Scotia. When he reached the age of fifteen, he became simply "Old Blue."

That dog, weighed down by folds of fat that nearly dragged the floor, was an affectionate creature. Rascoe and I thoroughly enjoyed slipping him food. Sadly, Old Blue died before the summer was out, trying to chase after a young female beagle passing by the restaurant, exuding canine sensuality and romance-provoking scent. The proprietor of Diana's told Rascoe and me that Old Blue had collapsed with a heart attack before he even reached the corner, that, tragicomically, the cute beagle never even saw his infatuated advance toward her from behind.

One morning over breakfast at Diana's, with Old Blue haunched beside our table (this was well before he died), waiting for handouts, Rascoe told me about some of his prison experiences. "I had a girlfriend named Shirley while I was in prison," he said. "She's from Toronto."

"You had a girlfriend while you were in prison?" My tone was incredulous.

"I did," replied Rascoe defensively, "through correspondence. I put an ad in a weekly advertising paper in Ontario saying I was in Dorchester and would like to correspond with a woman. I didn't say I was black. I got eleven replies...The one from Shirley developed into a long correspondence, into a romance. She sent me a photo of herself, and I thought she was one of the most beautiful women I'd ever seen."

"How long did this romance through correspondence go on?"

"Almost four years."

"The whole time you were in Dorchester?"

"Yes, just about. I received her first letter after I'd been in a couple months and we exchanged letters almost every day the first year. Then, when she entered the University of Guelph, the letters came only two or three times a week. She wanted to write more but didn't have time to write every day. I accepted that and limited my correspondence to replying to her letters, so that I didn't seem to be trying to force her to write more than she had time for. When I got a letter from her, I had a letter ready to go and I just added a couple paragraphs saying something specific about what she had written in her latest letter.

"The pattern was this: I'd respond the same day to letters I received from her and she needed three or four days for her reply, due to her studies and the time they took. I got to be a pretty good writer that way. I spent a lot of time educating myself. By reading a lot and improving my letters, I felt I was becoming more acceptable in her eyes."

My brows shot up. "More acceptable? If she accepted the fact that you're black and was willing to start a relationship knowing you were a con, I'm not sure I understand why you'd want to appear more 'acceptable in her eyes.'" I took a thoughtful swig of my coffee. "I can understand why you'd wanna be more educated and how writing might stimulate that and mesh with it, but I don't believe I understand this 'more acceptable in her eyes' stuff."

Rascoe peered at me as though I were clairvoyant. "You put your finger on it," he acknowledged. "I never told her I was black. I let the deception go on and on. I even sent her a photo of a friend, a white con in the next cell. I didn't want to lose her. I **needed** her. I **desperately needed** someone to write to on the outside, to give me something to hang onto, to give me a reason

77

to want to get out and go straight. I held on to her for dear life. I lived off her and her letters as much as I lived off the prison food I ate. She gave me the strength I needed to survive the hell of Dorchester."

"I see, I see," I said, beginning to see. "By conducting a pen-pal romance under the guise of being white, you not only survived, but you became more educated. But what of true love? Certainly the mere regular exchange of letters could not have continued four years on the strength of what you've described, not with an extremely attractive, young, nubile woman, that is. Some expression of love, some commitment to or hope held out for serious love, however obliquely, must have been made somewhere along the way."

"You're right. We did get serious. After two-and-a-half years of writing, Shirley suggested I propose to her. I was thrilled. A white woman in love with me! I was on Cloud Nine for days until I realized I could never tell her I was black, not after pretending to be white for so long. So I hedged, I needed her so bad. I said I didn't feel right proposing to her when I was still in prison, that I loved her too much to put her in that situation. I promised to propose to her when I was free and she accepted my promise. I guess she took what I had to say as about the same as a proposal."

"A distinction that stated a difference for you but not for her?"

Rascoe nodded. "Right."

"That is a real quandary, I can certainly see that, being in love, but yet afraid the real you isn't lovable."

Rascoe shrugged. "I kept on writing like I was white for another year, cuz I needed her even more as the years dragged on, as Dorchester more and more made me forget what it was like to be free and fully human, at least as human as a black man in Canada can be."

"Tough in there, I take it?"

"Very."

"Give me an example."

"Oh, like during a softball game, a guy got real angry and went after the pitcher with his bat. Soon everybody is swinging a bat or a fist, trying to hit someone on the opposing team."

"Did anyone get hurt?"

"Yeah. One guy sure got creamed. It was the umpire, some college kid from a university somewhere who was in Dorchester for the day to try and help us cons establish better rapport with people on the outside so we'd be better adjusted when we got out." Rascoe failed to stifle a sly grin. "The poor bugger didn't have enough sense to grab a bat or something to swing when the fighting broke out. He tried to stop the fighting. Someone knocked most his teeth out when he began yelling 'Stop it! This won't do! We are all in this together! Let's be peaceful!'" Rascoe's quote of the collegiate umpire was delivered in a comic simper, and I couldn't help but chuckle. "His mouth was split wide open," continued Rascoe, "and he was in hospital for a week." Rascoe smirked. "He never did return to ump the rest of that postponed game."

"He must've been naïve as hell."

"He was the most naïve and innocent little shit I ever saw. But he couldn't help it. He was just like the rest of those liberal college kids who think cons are the victims of their environment, culturally deprived, socially disadvantaged and all that bullshit. For a few cons that may be true, but a lot of them go into crime because they like that life -- the money, the danger, the whole nine yards. They love it. And why not? What is the alternative for them? Forty years working a conveyor belt in the Stanfield underwear factory up in Truro. That's the alternative, or something equally dead-end.

"They are willing to take what comes with a more exciting criminal career, including going to prison, because for them Dorchester is no worse than forty years making cotton-and-polyester briefs for Stanfield in a gloomy underwear factory where time is marked by the number of crotch covers you produce."

79

"You sound very familiar with Stanfield's underwear factory."

"I worked there over a year, until I couldn't take it any longer. I kept having bad underwear dreams, brief dreams that were long. They were always scary, but one night, my nightmare was real bad. A huge pair of extra-large blue Stanfield briefs flew out of the sky, followed by hundreds of others. Out the fly of each protruded a machine gun, and all those hundreds of blue Stanfield's dive-bombed me and fired on me, except they weren't firing bullets. They were pissing, pissing all over me, and I woke up screaming in a cold sweat. I knew I had finally reached the edge, that I might've already crossed over into the crazy zone. So, the next day I walked into the manager's office and quit and walked out with the pay they owed me."

"Holy shit. I didn't realize a factory job could get to someone that way."

"It did to me. I was too weak to stay with it then. Now I'm stronger. I want a future, to improve my mind especially, and I'm willing to make sacrifices, like work as a stock clerk downtown. I've grown up quite a bit during the years since I left Stanfield's. Dorchester had a lot to do with that, but mostly Shirley was the difference. Otherwise, Dorchester would've made me a hardened criminal, like it does a lot of them, rather than totally rehabbing me." Rascoe slipped a piece of bacon to Old Blue who wolfed it down with one easy, well-practiced, oleaginous gulp.

"Well, how did this thing with Shirley finally turn out?" I asked, slipping Old Blue a follow-up piece of bacon.

Rascoe puckered his lips tightly and his eyes shone pain and hurt. There was a sensitivity in those orbs I hadn't seen before. "Well, in the four years of our correspondence I could see that her letters were coming less and less often until I was lucky to get one a month." Rascoe's voice was cracking with the poignancy of his recollections. "Finally, I asked her what the fuck was going on, and she sent me one of those confessions, a 'true confession' I guess you'd call it. She said she'd become engaged to be married and that she'd have to stop writing. Her fiancé had found some of my letters and told her to stop writing the white convict in Dorchester. He said it was sick for a black woman to cozy up to a white criminal by writing love letters." Rascoe sighed deeply, the hard lines on his involuntarily expressive face telling me far more than his words how devastating the Shirley interlude in his life had ultimately proven. "She ended her last letter by apologizing to me for not telling me she was black. 'I should not have lied to you,' she wrote. 'It was wrong to string you along for four years like this for psychological reasons that are far from clear to me.'"

"Wow," I said. "Wow."

Rascoe looked ill after having told his story, as though his stomach was queasing about looking for a way out. He looked very pallid and peaked under his blackness and he began to absently feed the rest of his breakfast to a grateful Old Blue. "And you know what, Gary?" he went on.

"What?"

"Well, just a few weeks ago, I found where she got the picture she sent me. I found the exact same thing in a variety store on Barrington Street downtown. You can buy them for fifty cents." Rascoe focussed agate-hard eyes out the window at passers-by and traffic along Spring Garden Road.

"Buy what for fifty cents, for chrissake?" I asked impatiently.

"That damn woman sent me a picture of Hollywood actress Farrah Fawcett. I've seen her in that series, 'Charlie's Angels,' a few times since I got out of Dorchester. Inside, I did not have access to TV. I had to get out to find out that this con" -- Rascoe jabbed a thumb at his chest -- "had been thoroughly conned."

I stared sympathetically at Rascoe a few seconds and finally said, "If I were incarcerated in the pit of Dorchester, and someone sent me a picture of Farrah Fawcett, and said that was her, that her name was Shirley, I guess I'd fall in love, too. There wouldn't be much choice in the matter, as long as the lie would hold me together and keep me going."

Rascoe gave a small, bitter smile and exhaled forcefully, not at me, but at the world, and himself.

Halifax proved excellent birdwatching territory, especially the area around campus. I had arrived just in time for the tail-end of the warbler migration and I immediately set out to see as many of the stragglers as possible. Early in the morning, when warbler birding is best, I would often go to one of the city parks or I would look among the many trees and shrubs along the Haligonian streets.

One morning, just after daybreak, I became very excited when I spotted an unfamiliar bird tittupping through a tall ash tree on a residential street near campus. Ecstatically, I trained my binoculars on the small bird and watched it several minutes as it bobbed through the canopy of foliage. It was a beautiful blue bird. After I had a good look, I pulled out my field guide and consulted it, keeping a furtive eye on the warbler. I compared several warblers I'd seen before with the warbler in the ash tree, and identified him as the Black-throated Blue Warbler, all four inches of him. (The female of the species is not blue at all. She is a lackluster, drab-looking bird.) I gave a satisfied sigh. I could now enter the Black-throated Blue on my life list.

My Black-throated Blue flew out of the ash and into a viburnum beside a nearby house. I followed. I wanted to stay with my first Black-throated Blue as long as I could. Which I did. He was indeed even prettier amid the snow-ball clusters of small white flowers on the viburnum bush. Closer now, my binoculars gave me a spectacular, close-up view.

Suddenly I heard a shrill voice. "Jack, there is someone looking through my window with binoculars!"

I pulled away from my glasses and peered over them. Holy shit. My Black-throated Blue had warbled his sweet ass-feathers straight onto a bush that lined up with a young lady dressing in her bedroom. She had just apparently finished pulling on her baby-blue panties and had begun to halter herself with a lacy bra that was also of a delicate blue color. The woman had wrongly inferred that I was peeping at her when I was only absorbed in my very first Black-throated Blue Warbler. I hadn't even noticed the woman until she shrieked, and I certainly wasn't interested in her. I had seen plenty of her species before.

Well, I thought, such sticky situations can and do come along for a dedicated, aggressive birder seeking to add to his life list. Yet, certainly, to avoid further embarrassment for the young lady, I moved a few feet, and got a new angle on the viburnum, one that didn't include the young woman at her dressing table. God, that warbler was beautiful, a feast of both sight and sound. His unevenly cadenced tinkle of C-sharp notes piled one on another, broke briefly, then resumed for another high-pitched burst, over and over again. It was one of the most beautiful bird songs I'd ever heard. I had been looking for the Black-throated Blue for over a decade, and I was determined to remain rooted on that residential lawn zoomed in on that feathery wonder until he flew.

My doggedness proved a big, bird-brained mistake. The front door of the house suddenly swung open, and out ran the young lady's husband, "Jack," all six-foot-eight brawny pillar of him. He menacingly brandished an iron skillet, and there was hateful, fighting vengeance written on his face. In his tow came two comrades, not quite so large, but big. One carried a coffee pot and the other a cup of coffee. The three were dressed in green work trousers and brown workshirts, and they wore intimidating boondockers (the ones on the giant who was even bigger than me must've been 15 EE's). They looked like they did some pretty heavy work for a living, and that they were getting ready to leave for work. I nervously compared their horny hands to my soft, white academic, bird watching hands, and offered a timid smile which I hoped would deflect wrath.

From inside the house, the young woman cried, "Hit that Peeping Tom, you guys!"

I was a devout, dyed-in-the-feathers birder, but no kind of Peeping Tom! My bird watching had squeezed me into tight spots before -- like the time I was after a Wood Thrush under a ballpark bleacher at a woman's softball tournament -- but I had always managed to extricate myself through diplomacy. I felt confident I could handle this ominous situation, too.

I continued to smile as the three men approached, bristling with their weapons, dark, glowering expressions bedizening their weathered tanned faces. The intensity of their wrath contorted their faces into a kind of grotesqueness that was most alarming. And I could understand their feelings, too, the situation being what it was. "Good morning," I said brightly as the three prickly, blue-collar Haligonians arrayed themselves in front of me in a formidable phalanx. "Nice morning, isn't it?"

Big Jack challenged gruffly, "What the hell are you doing out here on my lawn watching my wife get dressed? She doesn't like it."

"I can explain, gentlemen," I offered pleasantly. "The reason for my presence here this morning is but an ornithological affair."

Big Jack's brow furrowed in puzzlement. "Ornery – thaw – logee – cal? Is that the same as pornographic?"

"Not at all. Ornithological is a word meaning, pertaining to birds, their identification, habitats, migratory patterns, and so forth. In point of ornithological fact, gentlemen," I smiled sheepishly, "I was bird watching."

Big Jack grunted, "I'll say you wuz! And the birdie you was watching is my wife, Duckie!"

"No, no," I corrected. "I was looking at a blue bird, not a duck!"

Big Jack's lips curled in huge disgust. "My wife's nickname is Duckie, you stupid Peeping Tom! Blue is Duckie's favorite color. All her lingerie is blue and she was putting it on when you were zooming in on her with your stupid-ass periscope. She was damn near naked, you creep!" He snarled viciously and stuck a fist in my face and from that fist flipped a finger at me (a new bird for me to look at!), three inches from my face. He gesticulated wildly, causing his bird to "fly" frenetically in

84

zigzagging intimidation in and out of the immediate environs of my nostrils. "If you want to look at a bird, look at this!" he yelled. "Take a good, final look at your last bird before I beat you to death!"

In dramatically gesticulating, Big Jack had inadvertently "flown" his bird straight up my right nostril. "Get your bird out of my nostril, please, sir," I complained in a furry, nasal voice.

Big Jack braced himself with the palm of his other hand against my face and with a tremendous heave pulled the bird free. "Christ that hurts!" I screamed. The "bird" free, I gave a nerve-jangled, placating smile and said "Thank you," and wet my Stanfield underwear. "Sorry about that bird that flew up your nose," quipped Big Jack gleefully. "You Peeping Tom!"

"No need to be angry, sir," I soothed, my nasal passage stinging. "The bird I was watching was not your wife. It was a Black-throated Blue Duckie, I mean Warbler."

"Don't joke about my wife Duckie, you goof," snarled Big Jack. Jack looked totally unconvinced that I was a birder, and he seemed ready to split my head open. But he gave me a chance to explain. "Show me your black-eyed blue bird!" he said acidly. "It's your last chance, your last hope to live. I never seen no black-eyed blue birds around here, ever before, not in my yard!"

I could see the warbler had left the viburnum and I could no longer hear its dulcet song. Nor did my cursory glancing about locate it. Desperately, I swept my arm toward the top of the ash tree and tried to sound genuinely enthused. "There he is," I shrilled. "See! See the bird! Isn't he beautiful?" I prayed the stratagem would work.

Big Jack squinted into the tree. "Where? Let me see with your periscope?"

I handed Big Jack my binoculars quicker than a warbler's heartbeat. He focussed them on the upper branches while his beautiful wife Duckie squawked from the porch, "Hit him, Jack! He's a Peeping Tom! Kill him dead and bury him out back!"

I decided to butter up to Big Jack in an attempt to counter the cries for my blood. I spoke in a confidential tone. "Actually Jack, though it is true that here this morning I'm but a mere birdwatcher, professionally I am Professor G. Louis Heath, internationally famous scholar. I'm here at Dalhousie University working on an important book. Close friends and the Prime Minister call me Gary. You can call me Gary, too."

Big Jack twirled the focus ring on my binoculars, in exasperation, trying to locate my bird, and muttered, "I'll call you Gary if I find the blue bird. If I don't, I'm gonna kill you, just like Duckie told me to! What Duckie says, I do!" Big Jack's two buddies glared at me and nodded their agreement.

I remembered my **Roger Tory Peterson Field Guide** in my left back pocket and my **Golden Field Guide** in the right. I pulled them out enthusiastically, with alacrity, alarming the two fellows who were covering me with a coffee pot and cup. "Easy," one warned darkly. "Don't do nothing foolish or you get it with these!" The pair gestured menacingly with the pot and cup, ready to attack.

I made my case to my tormentors, "Sirs, or should I say perhaps colleagues? -- indeed, fellow birders! -- these paperbacks are bird watching field guides. Are they not circumstantial evidence that the circumstances in which you have detected me are not what they seem?"

Big Jack pulled my binoculars away from his eyes, down to his chest. "Show me those friggin' birds! Show me the blue bird you say you were seeing!"

I displayed the color illustration of my warbler. "See!" I enthused. "Isn't he beautiful? And this morning is the first time I've ever seen him! Doesn't that make my indiscretion understandable?"

Jack examined the illustration as his wife yelled, "Put that damn book down, Jack! This is no time to be reading! Kill the son of a bitch! Bash his skull in and tee off on his balls, then bury him out back! If you don't put down that book right now -- what's he showing you, dirty pictures? -- and beat him to death in defense of my honor, you'll have hell to pay in this house, especially in the bedroom!"

I could see Big Jack's hostile expression changing to one of disgust as she shrilled. Duckie's latest salvo seemed to work a transformation in him. I could sense that, momentarily at least, I was no longer the enemy, and that he was even feeling a glimmer of sympathy for me in reaction to his wife's taunts. Big Jack turned his back to the porch so Duckie couldn't see he was grinning at me. "I can understand your problem, professor," he said under his breath, "but for future reference" -- he jerked his head slightly toward Duckie -- "I want you to know you aren't missing out on much even though the bird in the bush can look very inviting. Even a pretty little birdie can crap all over you."

I glommed promptly onto where Big Jack was coming from. Well, what the hell, I thought, any old way to get off this yard in one piece was fine and dandy with me. "Thank you most kind and beneficent sirs," I said in my most pitiful, heart-rending, soulful voice, as I sidled toward the sidewalk. "I am glad you understand my plight! Living in a room all summer, working on a dry, academic book" -- I managed to emit a woeful sob -- "well, you understand, I can see. So barren, so austere. I just had to get out and go bird watching this morning! I'm so glad you understand!" My voice had begun to take on a breathless quality, in order to elicit the maximum sympathy, allowing me to sidle the extra few yards I needed. "See you," I smiled as I reached the sidewalk.

I kept walking, smiling and waving over my shoulder, till I turned the corner. Then I ran like hell till I reached my residence hall on the Dalhousie campus.

Summer Expenses. I had had a difficult year financially when I arrived in Halifax and it was necessary that I live close to the bone that summer in order to be able to write full-time through August. As I traveled, the rents I paid for rooms reflected my straitened circumstances. For example: $5.50 for room 34 in the Hillsboro Hotel ("J.A. O'Leary, Clerk"), Pembroke, Ontario. Four dollars for a clean, modern, spacious room at the Université de Moncton, Moncton, New Brunswick.

87

(The clerk on duty was student Valmond Léger. "I am from Manitoba," he told me proudly. "Not here or Québec. People forget that there are French-Canadians in Manitoba. Vive Louis Riel!") Six dollars for room 2 at the Richland Hotel, Richland, Ontario, the filthiest room I have ever suffered anywhere.

And, in the States, $5.89 for the moldy, distempered walls of room 33 in the pee-stinking Grandview Hotel, Sault Ste. Marie, Michigan. $5.83 for room 223 in the old but clean General Pershing Hotel in roaring downtown Dubois, Pennsylvania. $6.24 for a mattress with a pendulous curve, much like a hammock, in room 52, Western Reserve Hotel ("Grace Serani, Clerk"), Ravenna, Ohio. $7.35 for room 7-B in the Kearsarge Hotel, Portsmouth, New Hampshire ("Sherman P. Newton, Jr., Mgr."). $8.00 for the absolutely terrible room 29 in the Park View Hotel, downtown Scranton, Pennsylvania. (After I'd returned from dinner, I had to drag a drunk sprawled before my door in order to get in.) And I shelled out $10.50 for lodging at the pleasant Northland Hotel at 38 Court Street, Houlton, Maine ("Your Host, The Adams Family"). The hotel featured an impressive, glistening white portico and inside it had recently been nicely redecorated in an eclectic, eighteenth century colonial style.

My Dalhousie University room, number 366 Bronson House, in Howe Hall, which occupied the northeast corner at the intersection of Coburg Road and Le Marchant, rented from an average $2.48 a night to $2.77, depending on whether the stupid or intelligent clerk was on duty when I paid. I arrived in Halifax June 12th, and for the period June 13th to June 30th I paid $50 for the room. For July 1 to August 17th, I paid $119. And for the one additional day I stayed beyond what I had originally planned, a last minute decision, I was charged $4.

I had my summer savings account at the Canadian Imperial Bank of Commerce, catty-corner from Howe Hall. Throughout seven summers in Canada, it was either the Canadian Imperial Bank of Commerce or the Bank of Montreal which nestled closest to the campuses I visited. And at Lakehead University in

Thunder Bay, Ontario (my 1978 summer), the Imperial Bank of Commerce had gone right onto campus, renting space in the University Centre.

My summer session parking sticker cost $5, a lot cheaper than the University of British Columbia's $11 sticker the previous summer.

For the historical record, I'd like to note that my 1974 Illinois license number was WG 1793. In a computerized world where each of us is, for all the world, a number, I'd like to proclaim that WG 1793 was a great number. It got me to Halifax and back to Normal, Illinois safely and comfortably. WG 1793 was always there for me throughout 1974.

I set a personal Canadian record that summer, attending sixteen movies at four Halifax theatres: Cove Cinema, Cinema Scotia Square, Odeon, and Paramount (all $2.50 admission). The first two are Canadian Famous Players Theatres.

The only Canadian film I saw, in Scotia Square, was "The Pyx," a Québec film about the ritual practice of black masses in a Montreal high-rise apartment building, on one of the highest floors, that on each occasion sacrificed the life of a young woman. "The Pyx" was the only Canadian film playing in Halifax that summer. It was a good movie, though a bit revolting to me personally. I regret there were not more Canadian movies available. I tired of viewing so much American cinema in Canada.

Seat 17, Row 4, Section 5, Halifax Forum. On June 21st, I paid $4 for a ticket (printed by "D. English & Co., Ltd., Montreal") which entitled me to sit in that seat the same day, in the afternoon, and watch Canada's All-Stars play basketball against China's best in two games, men's and women's. The Chinese women were surprisingly big. The Chinese women's center was, in fact, the tallest player on the court for the women's contest.

Both men and women Chinese players proved too mechanical in their play, methodically running plays to textbook perfection, failing to look for sudden opportunities to score.

When they finally did get off a shot, it was often a classic "set shot" that prevailed in U.S. college ball in the forties and early fifties. The Chinese lacked the finesse and magic, which the Canadians had, that comes from taking a basketball in your hands about the time you begin to walk, or even before, and building your skills from there. The two games devolved into good learning experiences for the Chinese, basketball clinics you might say. They quickly became yawners for the spectators who were spread sparsely through the Forum for an event televised across Canada.

Gas. I paid an average of 67.9 cents per Canadian gallon of regular. I paid Jack Topolinski Shell in Sudbury, Ontario $3.75 for 5.4 gallons and Yvon Gosselin Shell $2.50 for 3.4 gallons. Marcel Caron Shell in Riviere du Loup charged me $4.35 for 6.5 gallons and, at Gallagher's Shell in Fredericton, New Brunswick, it was $3.95 for 5.5 gallons. In Petitcodiac, New Brunswick, I handed the William L. Wade Shell Station $3.00 for 4.2 gallons. Golding's Tire Service in rural Woodstock, New Brunswick mugged me for $2.55 for 3.2 gallons and the Roland Davies station at 21 Queen Street in Truro, Nova Scotia ("Home Of The Stanfield Underwear Factory") held me up for $3.66 for 4.1 gallons. ("Pay in cash," joked the attendant, "or we'll stake you out in the mud flats and let the tidal bore drown you.")

The station I patronized most often was Bruce Flemming's Fina station in Halifax, at 6389 Quinpool Road, where Oxford Street intersects. It was one of Canada's best stations, a clean, friendly place that gave good service and charged reasonably -- 66.9 cents per Canadian gallon. I felt it worth driving out of my way to fill up at that service centre.

I dined several times in the cafeteria of the Izaak Walton Killam Children's Memorial Hospital near campus. I often talked with parents who had children in the hospital. Stan and Ethel were the most memorable. Their eleven-year-old son, Ian, suffered from a rare, painful disease, which translates from the

Latin roughly as a "softening of the bones" -- one of a number of such diseases, and Ian's was the rarest. Stan said it was the most painful and lethal type. "There have only been three cases ever in Canada." The disease caused Ian to frequently break bones, and they healed very slowly. For his fractures he had to be hospitalized, his entire body immobilized, and surgery performed, if he was to have any chance at all. The danger was that marrow would massively escape his bones and cause a heart attack and quick death.

It was Ian's fourteenth visit to the Killam. Stan and Ethel looked like they had all the world upon their shoulders. In retrospect, what amazes me, is that they talked to me at all. Their faces were so haggard and drawn. I didn't try to open up a conversation even though they were seated at my table in the cafeteria, only a couple seats down the long imitation mahogany, and we were the only diners at the table. I recognized their suffering and kept to myself. Yet Stan spoke to me, thinking I too had a child in Killam. That's what he asked about, and I told him I was at the University for the summer, writing a book. More bits of conversation were traded and soon we moved together, I scooting to them at their request.

We talked almost two hours, about a variety of things, but mostly about their son Ian and themselves. It was a surprisingly pleasant conversation, given the place and the occasion that prompted Stan and Ethel to be there. It was about the only time the divorced couple got together. "It's hard to pinpoint exactly why we divorced," said Ethel, "but for sure it was mostly the bone disease. The disease fundamentally altered the relationship we had, and after a while we realized we could no longer remain married...If we didn't also have Max, our other son, who is healthy, maybe the marriage would've survived. I think what did it for me was trying to be a mother in two worlds. The strain was terrible. I can't imagine going to war and feeling any more strain. At least there you have one enemy. I had two fronts to fight on, raising one well son to be an adult and assisting another to die as comfortable a premature death as possible, yet still trying to keep him alive as long as possible..."

Stan also spoke at length. "I got Max, the healthy son, in the divorce settlement and she got Ian. We, of course, have full visitation rights, both of us, to the kid the other's got." Stan smiled thinly at Ethel. "We remain friends, like buddies who have been through a war and get together for reunions. But our love is dead. If I learned anything, other than a lot about a rare bone disease and how to take care of it and adjust my life to it, it's a fact that I didn't fully realize before. And that's that a beautiful love relationship can die, irretrievably, when it has to survive in a drastic, new situation.

"That's why we fought so much before we split up permanently. We had become chained together unnaturally where before we were bonded together through love and the two sons borne of that love, Max and Ian. But when Ian began to be destroyed, so did we. The marriage died, and now the only thing that brings us together are the visits to the hospital for Ian. When he dies, there will be no more friendship. We may even each find someone else to marry...Certainly Max won't bring us physically together. I'll just send him to her on a bus for his visits. He's getting old enough for that. He's almost twelve..."

This is so very, very sad, I thought. I am over in room 366 Bronson House, Howe Hall, writing an arid tract about one of the New Left groups that think with dry ideas that were given to them in little boxes when I could be considering the pain of real life such as that so poignantly borne in on me at this long table in the cafeteria of Izaak Walton Killam's Children's Hospital.

Real life does not fit into neat little boxes. The pain and complexity and love and caring and dying of which it is comprised, and the myriad other nuances and "things" too, for want of a better word, that are the mysterious, unfathomable experience of Stan and Ethel, as mysterious and unfathomable as their original love story, defy characterization and interpretation with theories, footnotes, research studies, or any other academic hogwash you might attempt to paint it with to make it more intelligible and accessible to the mind. Their experience was not so. Their experience was at its core religious, beyond reason, almost beyond belief. They had asked, "Why is this happening to us?" In trying to respond to this question, they were tugged to a higher level of existence, more removed from the immediate sting of their pain, where spirit might grow and be nourished as Ian moved toward his inevitable fate through progressive surgeries. Through it, I sensed they had built the spiritual power to see Ian through to the most meaningful child's grave possible, to confer a sense of eternity to his dying. They knew, and said as much to me, that, though the order of things is usually reasonable, when it was not so for them, they seized the opportunity as best they could to create a larger dimension to their lives. They told me they initially felt totally inadequate to deal with the challenge Ian presented, but they had managed to move on. I felt really good after my lengthy conversation. I felt spiritually at ease in the presence of the immense inner glow that their supreme struggle had kindled.

A war party of Ojibwa Indians made national headlines that summer by seizing Anicinabe Park near Kenora, Ontario, and throwing up barricades of picnic tables and benches tied loosely together with barbed wire. Brandishing tomahawks, bows, high-powered rifles, and Molotov cocktails, their faces streaked with yellow and red war paint, a huge leather drum throbbing in the background, they presented a formidable group as they looked into "The National" evening newscast's cameras and defied the government. Their leader, Chief Cameron, proclaimed the park "liberated Indian territory." "This land, this park," he shrilled, "is something the Department of Indian Affairs bought in 1929 with **our** money and then used it for their own selfish purposes. That money was supposed to be kept in trust for us!" Chief Cameron's face contorted bitterly. "Then in 1959, the damn crackers sold this" -- he swept his arm over the park -- "to the Kenora town council. It was all very evil, and very illegal!" The

Chief raised a clenched fist toward the camera. We demand the park be returned! We demand this be done by five p.m. Friday! We want our land back! We must have it to survive as a nation!"

The CBC later interviewed Kenora Mayor Jim Davidson, who spoke in the tones of an oily Babbitt, yet spoke sense. "I have met with the town council. They, we, will be very pleased to discuss all issues fully with the Indians. We are only interested in justice in this matter. But we cannot talk seriously looking down the barrel of a gun. We won't have anything to do with violence. Accordingly, we have decided we cannot carry on any kind of meaningful negotiations with the Ojibwa until they have left Anicinabe Park. And for starters, we **demand** they get their weapons out of the park immediately."

The federal government, for its part, took the position that outside agitators -- especially Dennis Banks, who had been a leader the year before at the Wounded Knee insurrection in South Dakota -- had organized the occupation for their own selfish, publicity purposes and that the local Ojibwa would be best advised to give up the park and "avail themselves of the appropriate channels for redress of grievances." Ottawa made it abundantly clear that it, like the town council, would never negotiate under the threat of violence.

In response, Chief Cameron noted that the "appropriate channels" had never proved more to the Ojibwa than an endless treadmill of red tape, leading nowhere, and that the warpath had become their last hope.

What eventuated was that, over several days, Indian solidarity fractured. Internal bickering shattered morale and a stream of defectors reduced the occupying force to a mere 64. Finally, Chief Cameron realized the whites had counted coup on him, and rather than make things even worse, he laid down his tomahawk and rifle and led his acrimonious band out of Anicinabe.

Knots of hostile whites stood by as the Ojibwa exited. Chief Cameron stopped to make a brave, brief show to the media, announcing he had postponed his deadline for Kenora to cede the park to his people. He explained that he had done so in order to first have an opportunity to negotiate with town officials. But the message that his drawn, fatigued visage conveyed was that the Ojibwa occupation of Anicinabe had been broken.

A national election campaign brought Prime Minister Pierre Trudeau to Halifax to speak at the Bayers Road Shopping Centre. Rascoe and I attended the speech, standing far back in the crowd of about a thousand. The PM had drawn a good crowd, considering he was stumping in the diehard-conservative home riding of the man he was campaigning against, Progressive Conservative Party leader Robert Stanfield, scion of the Stanfield Underwear Dynasty. I liked the laid-back, festive air of that throng, featuring a wide array of clothing, including a few bathing suits (men's and women's) and one woman in a pastel-pink housecoat and matching fake-fur scuffs on her feet and plastic curlers in her hair. Most every man was clad casually, something like Rascoe and me, which was to say, in short-sleeve summer shirts and doubleknit polyester casual slacks. Rascoe wore suede jogging shoes and I had on canvas tennis shoes.

Most the women wore breezy, bright blouses or tank tops and skirts, slacks, or shorts, all of summer weight. Sandals predominated under the soles of the women.

Mothers were there comforting crying babies in their arms, crooning and cooing soothing words, and school-age children had appeared in force. A good number scampered about eating ice cream, cotton candy, and peanuts, and washing all that down with soft drinks their parents had bought from vendors working the crowd. The older children, the teens, stood around listlessly, their shoulders hunched in a mixed message of defiance and aimlessness, their expressions a blend of the cynical and the lazy, and certainly their bodies mature enough for rebellion, vandalism, mayhem, and prison. A few gave off a strong scent of grass and booze, which had already escalated some of them into profound highs.

95

G. Louis Heath, Ph.D.

The platform erected on the mall parking lot for the PM was decked out with red and white bunting and colorful campaign posters. Trudeau stood ramrod erect, a smiling vulpine expression on his face. He was a towering eminence, who impressed me greatly with his acute charm and rapport, his power and his charisma, which supported an invisible, yet virtually palpable bridge between him and the crowd.

Flanking Trudeau were supporters, mostly prominent people, seated in folding chairs. After thanking the people who had prepared for his visit to Halifax, the Prime Minister launched into a criticism of the Tories, characterizing Stanfield's proposed program of wage and price controls as "a proven disaster looking for a place to happen." (After he was re-elected, Trudeau implemented a very similar program of controls himself, another instance of a liberal politician bringing off with ease the implementation of a conservative proposal.) He next attacked Québec's Bill 22, which made French the exclusive, official language of Québec. He insisted, "Each province must be genuinely bilingual for Confederation, for **our Canada**, to survive, and for all of us to prosper."

Trudeau eloquently ticked off his campaign promises. Subsidized interest rates. $500 grants for first-time home buyers. Massive aid to urban transit. Federal takeover of railway passenger service. Guaranteed income for the disabled. Legislation requiring the disclosure of interest rates.

Rascoe made a sour face and said under his breath, "He gives us this crap every time he runs, but none of his promises ever come true. Hell, if there were enough ex-con niggers like me, he'd even promise us something, if we could vote." Rascoe snickered disgustedly. "He'd be promising guaranteed incomes for ex-con niggers, urban transit for ex-con niggers, and $500 grants for one-time-loser, ex-con niggers!" Rascoe gave a snort of vehement revulsion, as much a snuffled exhalation really, a lengthy one, as a snort.

"You're just bitter, that's all," I whispered.

"Shhhhh. Shhhhhhh," returned Rascoe with an upraised, shushing index finger, as though I had started the exchange while the PM addressed the crowd, and as if I were the too-loud one. "Let the Prime Minister finish, Gary," admonished Rascoe. "The idiot may have something to say!"

"And finally I say to you," continued Trudeau, "I am a good man and a good leader. I can do the job. I am doing the job. Help give me the clear majority I need to carry out my policies. We need especially to stimulate the economy here in Halifax-Dartmouth. To achieve that goal, I need your votes on election day!" The Prime Minister lifted his arms high over his head and smiled broadly. "With your help, we can win!"

The crowd gave Trudeau a loud, prolonged applause, laced with adulatory cheers, and Rascoe smiled wide and raised his arms in imitation of the PM. "With your help, we can win!" he simpered, turning to me. "There's a crock for you, Gary! Can you dig that con artist, eh?"

"Shhhhh," I reproved. "He's looking our way." Which is to say, Trudeau was looking in our general direction as he posed with local campaign people for photographs.

As we walked from the mall parking lot where Prime Minister Trudeau had given his speech, I could see that the crowd had deposited considerable litter. Candy wrappers, popcorn, torn-up posters, cigarette butts, all the usual detritus a large crowd leaves in its wake was copiously strewn about. "It's not a clean election," I quipped. "So much trash these people leave behind. It looks like the aftermath of a three-day rock festival in upstate New York or central Illinois. Gross."

"White people in the Maritimes are **so trashy!**" exclaimed Rascoe, spreading his arms theatrically over the lot and drawing a good number of puzzled and offended stares from those near us. "It really disgusts me. I wish they'd clean up their act!" Rascoe wadded up his ice cream wrapper and hurled it, narrowly missing a group of three women. When the wad landed at their

97

feet, they looked around for the child who had thrown it, but could not find him, because Rascoe had hauled in his hand quickly and resumed walking at my side, his face a study in perfect innocence. "That black trash I threw," he said **sotto voce,** "mixed in with all this white trash, is the most integration we have here in Halifax. It's as good as it gets. Take that from Rascoe who grew up in Halifax's all-black Africville not far from here, a small shantytown, three streets of it, near the Bedford Basin."

    While I was in Halifax, United Nations Secretary-General Kurt Waldheim, fearing war on Cyprus, urged Canada to double its peacekeeping force on the island. After a two-day Cabinet debate, External Affairs Minister Mitchell Sharp announced Canada would send 450 additional men to join the 488 troops already on Cyprus, to meet the UN request, but also in order to beef up Canadian strength so that they could better protect themselves. Twelve Canadian soldiers had recently been wounded because the strength of the UN forces was proving inadequate to police Cyprus and enforce the ceasefire. Mitchell Sharp wanted no more of that. The troops he promised were quickly sent.

    I watched TV news coverage of the 450 soldiers in the Canadian Airborne Regiment boarding planes in Edmonton. A CBC reporter spoke with two soldiers in fatigues and berets as they waited to climb into their aircraft. An olive-complected stripling about age twenty, sporting a pencil-thin mustache, hailed from a northern Québec village with a lengthy name. He owned a French surname equally as long. "I am proud to go to Cyprus," he said in halting English. "A good mission for a soldier, to keep peace." Another infantryman, blond, about twenty, nervously gave "The National" reporter his very English surname and hometown, Sussex, New Brunswick. His mouth glimmered, a geode of silver fillings, as he spoke. "Well, this is very sudden for sure, eh. I didn't expect, I didn't think I'd be going anywhere like Cyprus this soon. But I'll do my best, the best I can, eh." He shrugged a little and gave a small, involuntary grimace. "Orders are orders, eh?"

Bulging duffel bags hefted onto their shoulders, the men boarded a C-130 Hercules and a 707 superjet with machine-like discipline. A sparse crowd waved as the planes filled, and soon the sleek, camouflage-painted planes were airborne, drab dots in the brilliant Alberta azure, winging toward the necropolis of Nicosia.

Before I left Halifax, twenty-nine of the men in those planes had become casualties. Nine of those were deaths, Canadians killed by Syrian antiaircraft guns which mistook a Canadian Armed Forces Buffalo Transport for the enemy. I thought of the crying and disbelief, the mourning and the grief, as the tragic news of the deaths reached homes in outport Newfoundland, rural Québec and New Brunswick, small-town Manitoba, and other points throughout Canada, and I felt profoundly saddened.

The TV room played a much less important role in my life in Halifax than the previous summer in Vancouver. But Howe Hall did have a lively, more intelligent TV crowd, and I occasionally joined them. The "night porter," nicknamed "Old Bill," a retiree from Saskatchewan, put in at least one visit to the TV room every night. He had a very full head of hoary white hair and a very pale face owing to health problems. Old Bill liked to lustily sing "Roll On Saskatchewan" and tell hilarious jokes. Always a lot of fun, he was a favorite of the TV crowd.

One evening in August, Old Bill failed to appear for work. We were told that he had been stricken by a heart attack that morning, and had died that evening, about the time his shift was to begin.

We were deeply saddened at the passing of our friend, the blustery, raucous old swaggerer from the Prairie, a very off-the-wall personage whose eccentricities compelled your attention and warmed you to him. A victim of the hard times before social programs were created to help the poor, he had made shift during the 1930s and survived by raising chickens, sheep, and cows, and cultivating a small truck garden, a few miles outside Estevan, Saskatchewan. He managed to keep himself, his wife, and five children eating through the twelve years between steady jobs. Old Bill was a study in pioneer-style self-reliance who presented to the world a doughty, tough persona, though at his core he was a gentle, deeply spiritual person. He read Scripture regularly in the early wee hours, on a job that proved to be the last leg of his terrestrial journey.

I made the acquaintance of Dr. John Lee, a professor of physics from Prince Edward Island University, who was staying on the first floor of Howe Hall and doing research at Dalhousie that summer. We took a few walks together, mostly down Spring Garden Road through Halifax Gardens, the most beautiful public park I visited in Canada, rivaled only by the one in Windsor, Ontario. Mount Royal Park in Montreal and Stanley Park in Vancouver are bigger, very impressive, but not nearly so nice. They are, in fact, scuzzy places compared to pristine Halifax Gardens, which are patrolled during the day to stop vagrancy cold and are surrounded by a tall, wrought-iron fence that is locked at night.

On our walks, Dr. Lee and I conversed lengthily. He had recently been divorced from his much younger wife, and that, of course, was weighing heavily on his mind. "My marriage fell apart partly because of Charlottetown. It's a small town and there just wasn't enough for my wife to do. She was used to the life of Ottawa, where she's from, and I had to keep figuring out things for her to do to keep her busy and happy. Our little boy was just not enough to fill her life...She is a good mother and I know our four-year-old son will have a good situation in Ottawa with her...She comes from a wealthy family where jewels, furs, fine cars, the expensive things of life, are taken for granted...I met her at a big dance in Ottawa, where I took my doctorate, at

Carleton University. She was the most beautiful woman at the dance, and I felt very flattered when she showed an interest in me…Part of the problem from the beginning was that I married her when she was only nineteen and I was almost thirty. There was too much of a gap. We were at different stages in our lives."

John also told me something of Prince Edward Island University. "To tell you the truth, Gary, though it sounds a little vain, I have published more than the rest of the Arts and Science faculty combined…The older profs are very threatened by me, and they tried to deny me tenure, but I won out…I'm able to do good research despite problems, and PEIU is getting better and better as new people are hired and the deadwood retires or dies off…The campus is very beautiful and we have an excellent administration that is building the best university possible…I'm happy I went to PEI, though someday I hope my research takes me to a more prestigious school. But times are so tough now for Ph.D.s in physics that everyone is staying put."

John and I tried to collaborate as scientist and writer. The idea was for me to help him put his scientific findings into good, popular, written form. But that effort fell flat on its face because I couldn't understand much of what he was saying. After John became frustrated at our joint efforts one afternoon, I mumbled something about "finishing for the day," and that "it's been a good session," and we desisted from our tomfoolery, never to resume.

In October, John traveled from Dalhousie, not back to PEI, but on to a sabbatical at Hong Kong University. He sent me an aerogramme dated February 25, 1975: "My research goes well," he wrote, "and I anticipate several articles coming out of it…I have had a number of dates with some very nice young Chinese women. My money will run very low before I get back to PEI, but this sabbatical is worth it, both professionally and personally."

101

Shortly before I left Halifax, I looked around for an authentic souvenir of all Canada, not just Halifax or Nova Scotia. At the time, I felt that Halifax would be my last summer in Canada. I had done the country from B.C. to the Maritimes. Only a summer teaching job would bring me back and I anticipated nothing opening up. So, I began a search for the quintessentially unique, authentic, All-Canadian Souvenir, something to remember Canada by once the avalanche of years had dimmed my memories.

I visited every shop and department store in town that I felt possibly could have a Canadian souvenir, but found nothing. As a last resort, I went into a T-shirt boutique in Scotia Square and began looking over shirts with a wide array of illustrations and photo reproductions silk-screened on. I considered those shirts rather gaudy, but I was so desperate for a souvenir, I thought they might have one with a nice Canadian theme or motif. Just so there was something Canadian about it, I'd purchase it.

The faces of Hollywood stars and British rock stars adorned many shirts. Mick Jagger, John Lennon, Elton John, Farrah Fawcett, Robert Redford, The Bionic Man, Spiderman, The Bionic Woman, The Incredible Hulk, and Superwoman (Lynda Evans) were especially in evidence on shirts. Suggestive messages such as "Nurses Do It Better" and "I Am Where The Action Is" emblazoned others. But, in all the bins and on all the shelves I searched, I could find nothing Canadian.

I left the boutique in Scotia Square and wandered along Barrington Street until I found a dimestore, which I entered. I approached the first clerk I saw. "Show me your Canadian souvenirs. I wanna buy one."

The sexagenarian, blue-rinsed woman smiled kindly and led me down a nearby aisle, full of novelty items. She stopped about halfway down and turned toward me, her lips pursed primly, her nose slightly aloof, and her hands folded together over her massive, craggy bust. "This is our Canadian section," she informed me rapturously.

"Point to the Canadian stuff," I said, delighted. "I can't locate it right off."

"Right in front of me," she returned, "about two feet above my head." She stepped onto a footstool and grabbed two items, a porcelain cup adorned with a Canadian flag and an extruded plastic figurine of a Mountie. "These are true Canadian mementos!" she gushed.

When I saw what she had, I went crazy out of my mind with ecstasy. "I finally got what I want!" I exulted. "Wrap them up. I'll take them both!"

After I returned to Illinois in late August, I placed the Mountie on my mantle and I began drinking coffee from the cup. Soon I discovered the following on the bottom of the cup: "National Flag of Canada, No. 3303. JAPAN." That discovery prompted me to step to the mantle and inspect the base of the Mountie whose plinth read, **"CANADA."** Upending the Mountie, I found the very depressing inscription underneath, **"MADE IN HONG KONG, NO. 205."** My All-Canadian Souvenir had feet of Hong Kong!

My chagrin over this provoked me to write a poem expressing my disappointment:

The Imported Canadian National Anthem

O Canada!
O Plastic Mountie!
"Made in Hong Kong, No. 205"
O Canada!
Hail the Oriental coffee cup!
"National Flag of Canada,
No. 3303. JAPAN."
O Canada!
O say can you see!
From sea to sea!

103

We'll never chip you.
We'll never scratch you.
We stand on guard for thee!
From the Maritimes to B.C.
Even in Québec and on the Prairie
We stand on guard for thee!
Oh Canada!

Chapter 4

University of New Brunswick, 1975

In the late fall of 1974, I did my usual. I applied to all the universities in Canada where I hadn't taught. The only school to reply encouragingly in the early going was the University of Saskatchewan at Saskatoon. In fact, after a lengthy correspondence, they led me to expect a formal job offer any day. Instead, to my total surprise, I received a letter asking if I spoke both French and English fluently.

I replied that I had had six years of French, four in high school, two at the University of California, and that I'd passed the French exam for Ph.D. candidates at Berkeley. I reported, however, that I had a very limited ability to converse in the language. And that ended that in Saskatoon.

Ironically, I was eventually hired to teach the summer of '75 in Canada's most bilingual province, New Brunswick. The University of New Brunswick at Fredericton never even brought up the issue of French. Why should they? Their courses were taught in English, the same as those at Saskatoon, and, besides, it was only a five-week summer position they were hiring me for. UNB sought diligently for bilingualism in their full-time faculty, yet only admired it in their summer professors.

(To jump ahead briefly to the next chapter: Even more ironically, I was hired to teach the next summer, 1976, at what amounted, very loosely translated, to a branch campus of the University of Saskatchewan, namely, the up-and-coming University of Regina, located in beautiful Regina, the capital city of Saskatchewan, from which presumably flow provincial interpretations and enforcement of federal bilingual policy. Apparently, something went drastically awry, and Saskatoon effectively seceded from the province in the matter of bilingual policy.)

105

From the University of New Brunswick, I received the following letter, dated November 8, 1974:

Dear Professor Heath,

We are delighted that you are interested in offering Foundations courses at our annual summer session.

Unfortunately, the knife has fallen and we are unable to offer as many courses in this area as we would like. I am enclosing a calendar* copy for two courses: EDUC 5321 Comparative Education and EDUC 5-6861 The School and Society. We hope you will offer to teach these courses for us.

Please do not be disturbed with the description of the Comparative courses which suggest comparison of the New Brunswick system. We are quite sure that with your vast experience and knowledge, the comparative nature of the course should become global. I am sure the New Brunswick students will offer you many details of their system.

I am enclosing two Course Information Forms which you should complete and return to me as quickly as possible.

Yours very truly,

Henry E. Cowan
Assistant Professor
Coordinator, Faculty of Education Summer Session

Enclosures

(*The Canadian "calendar" is what we in American universities and colleges call a "catalogue.")

I considered the course descriptions Professor Cowan had xeroxed from the UNB calendar for me: **EDUC 5321, Comparative Education**, 3 credit hours. A comparison of the New Brunswick system of education with systems of education in the other provinces, the British Isles and in certain other countries; and, **EDUC 5-6861, The School and Society**, 3 credit hours. A study of the interrelationship between the school and society. This course will seek to analyze the social forces influencing schools, students, and the direction of education.

I knew I could teach these courses well. So, I wrote Cowan that I was accepting his offer. On December 5th, he wrote back to confirm my appointment:

Dear Dr. Heath,

We are delighted that you have accepted our offer to teach at Summer Session, 1975. Please accept this as a formal offer of appointment to the Summer Session Faculty.

I have directed the Summer Session and Extension Office to forward a contract to you as soon as possible.

Should you require further assistance from us, do not hesitate to write.

■■■

Below is a copy of the contract I signed:

THE UNIVERSITY OF NEW BRUNSWICK EXTENSION AND SUMMER SESSIONS	**Distribution of Form**
	White - Director
	Green - Department Head
CONFIRMATION OF SESSIONAL APPOINTMENT	Blue - Dean
	Pink - Appointee

107

OFFER OF APPOINTMENT

The University of New Brunswick offers the following appointment to:

Mr.	HEATH	GARY	LOUIS
	(surname)	(first)	(middle)

Mailing Address: Department of Curriculum and Instruction, Illinois State University, Normal, Illinois, USA 61761

Session: SUMMER SESSION   Faculty: EDUCATION

Position Offered: Lecturer
Campus or Centre: FREDERICTON
Commencing: July 4, 1975   Ending: August 9, 1975
Salary: $2,200   Payment Details: single payment – August 9, 1975
Specific Duties to be Performed: TEACH: EDUC 5321 – Comparative Education and EDUC 5-6861 - The School and Society
Special Conditions (if applicable):
                Travel Allowance - $300.00 (maximum)
Dated: 1 December 1974   Offered by: (signed) T. F. Morris, Director, Summer Sessions

Note: After signing, appointee should retain the pink copy and return the remaining copies to: Director of EXTENSION AND SUMMER SESSIONS, ROOM 125, MACLAGGAN HALL, UNB, FREDERICTON, NB, CANADA.

I taught School and Society from 8 to 9:50 A.M. and Comparative Education from 10 to 11:50 A.M. daily, Monday through Friday. Forty-five were enrolled in School and Society and 52 in Comparative Education, a class so large that it had to be re-assigned to the D'Avray Hall auditorium. No such luck as I had had in British Columbia, but at least I was not desperately ill as I was on Point Grey.

My 8 a.m. School and Society class was comprised mostly of New Brunswick administrators and teachers who had squared off against one another a couple months earlier in what the teachers' union had termed a "work-to-rule campaign," a job action in which the teachers expressed their disgust with low salaries by doing only what they were absolutely required to do. They refused to stay one second past the end of classes, switch off lights, right toppled waste baskets, intervene in fights, counsel students, and so forth.

One working-to-the-rule tenth-grade teacher in my class, Byron, had even refused to speak to his class. Each day he showed a sequence of films to his World History class without introduction or comment, eventually unreeling his school's entire film library to fill up the school year. The kids loved the films, and they loved his class, because he never assigned homework or gave tests and everyone got an excellent grade. Certainly, Byron had his qualms. "I hated to do this," he acknowledged. "It was sort of malfeasance when I think back on it, but I'm not so sure that I and the others who boycotted teaching by showing films wouldn't do it again. We didn't want to strike, but we had to let the government know in a dramatic way how much we were hurting financially. We were 40 percent behind the other provinces. So you can see when we did get an increase to achieve something approaching parity, it was a big one. That is why I and some others in here are getting increases for taking this one course of yours that exceed what you're getting paid to teach it. Our new salary schedule really is jumping us far up there for very little additional scholarity if we're on the right place on the schedule." Byron paused and sighed, a little sadly. "But even for that 40 percent I still feel bad. In fact, I'm feeling worse all the time about showing films to my classes for weeks on end and never even speaking to them."

A high school principal, Walt, glared at Byron, then skimmed his eyes over the class. "You may've gotten your big increase," he said, "but you sure did cause us administrators a lot of grief. The kids knew you teachers weren't doing your job and they got pretty sloppy in their behavior. Some got downright wild. When some of you made movie theatres out of your classes, and pulled that other stuff you pulled, a lot of the kids felt free to do things they normally wouldn't try -- vandalism, fighting, profanity, tardiness, unexcused absences, stealing. This past spring was the hardest part of my career as a school administrator, I can tell you that for sure."

A hand shot up in the gentle breeze wafting through the windows from off the St. John River that flows through downtown Fredericton. It was Denny, a local high school teacher. "Walt, I've been hearing a lot about a teacher in your school, an art teacher, who during the work-to-rule, had her students sketch her while she posed nude on a stool and read from the Bible. Everybody's been talking about her. What was that all about, eh?"

Walt grimaced. "You would have to bring that up. I've filed a formal school complaint against her. I want to discipline her as severely as I can." Walt's voice rose angrily. "If she doesn't agree to retire -- she's sixty-four -- I want to have her terminated. She is undergoing psychiatric evaluation now and retirement looks like where she's headed."

My Comparative Education class of 52, the largest I ever had in Canada, included twelve Kenyans, all industrial technology majors. They had recently arrived in the country under the sponsorship of CIDA, the Canadian International Development Agency.

The Kenyans initially found it difficult to understand my rapid-fire English. Three of them, Isaac Ominde, Francis Wambugu, and Pelirson M'njaria came to my office after the first class. M'njaria gave me a woebegone look and said in a very sad voice, "Sir, we did not understand one word today. You speak very fast. It is too fast for us." He smiled and asked brightly, "Is it not possible for you to speak more slowly?"

I smiled back at M'njaria. "Certainly," I replied. "I'm sorry about speaking so fast. I did not realize it would be so difficult for you to understand. But I see the situation now. I am glad you came in here and told me about this. I want you to learn as much as possible in my class. From here on out," -- I was already enunciating more deliberately -- "I shall be very careful to slow down so that you can follow me."

The three smiled broadly, and Ominde added, "Sir, is it possible for you to tutor us after class? We are new in Canada and we can use extra help. The textbook is most difficult for us. Also your first homework assignment."

I agreed to tutor as much as they needed it. I didn't realize what I was getting into because I ended up tutoring several of the Kenyans at least an hour a day the entire six-week summer session. But, for the most part, I enjoyed it. The Kenyans were eager learners who worked very hard.

One afternoon, I told the Kenyans, "The world is changing so fast, it is difficult to predict what the relationship between Kenya and North America will be in a hundred years. Certainly, Kenya will be one of the 'have nations' of Africa. You will be a wealthy, well-developed, prestigious country and your children and grandchildren will not be coming to Canada to take courses because you will have your own universities that will be among the best in the world."

Wambugu grinned and observed, "Africa was the cradle of civilization. We once led the world and we shall do it again. Kenya is building a society today that will be one of the world's best. This is what Jomo Kenyatta wanted. This is why we broke from Britain, why we had our revolution and sent their Viceroy packing. The happiest day in my life was, as a boy, when my father took me to the airport to watch Kenyatta put that racist cracker Viceroy on a plane bound for London."

111

M'njaria smiled. "We are ahead of Canada that way. They still have not thrown the British out."

Another day, in class, the most talkative, acerbic, and eloquent Kenyan, Simon Wanami, had the following exchange with Rachel Wilson about women's liberation, a topic that had come up during a discussion of women's roles in Third World societies' educational systems:

Wanami: "Women's liberation is nonsense. The place of the woman is to give her man children, to raise them, and serve and adore him. It is written so in the Bible. I come from a family with eighteen children -- eleven boys, seven girls. My father is a real man. My mother is a real woman."

Wilson: "No way! Women must have professional identities! Raising a child or two is fine, eh, but only if you work too. Otherwise, it's degrading, just cleaning up after children and a husband, and doing all the shit work!"

Wanami: "Are you married?"

Wilson: "No, not yet."

Wanami: "How old are you?"

Wilson: Bristles silently.

Wanami: "You are forty if you are a day. Face it, woman, you are ugly like an old, old cow. You are a woman freedom fighter because no man will have you! If you cannot have a man, then you can have liberation. Isn't that it?"

Wilson: "You are trying to put words in my mouth! I'm not married by choice. I'm too busy with my career for men."

Wanami: "You mean you gave up happiness in order to do things such as enroll in Dr. Heath's course?"

Wilson: "That's a small part of it, Dr. Heath's class, if you want to look at it that way."

Wanami: "Indeed, this course is excellent," he said with a wry grin. "Dr. Heath is a most excellent lecturer. But in Kenya, society has not deteriorated so much that women think school is more interesting than sex!" A good number in the class burst into laughter.

Wilson: "Maybe if enough Kenyans came to school in Canada, Kenya would eventually enter the twentieth century and Kenyans would stop counting wives along with their chickens and cattle."

Wanami: "What we hope to teach Canada is that the more wives you have, the more cattle, chickens, and pigs you can take care of."

Wilson: "You are a male, chauvinist pig!"

Wanami beamed triumphantly, "Yes, but I am a man first!"

Wanami's brazen assertiveness was remarkable given the grave threats to the Kenyans that existed in the community. No other Kenyan was anywhere near as outspoken as Simon Imbefu Wanami, and he was very careful only to express himself freely on campus. The twelve Kenyans were well aware that an African had recently been slain near campus and that a Ku Klux Klan-style cross had been burned on the lawn in front of the residence hall where most the Kenyans stayed. They stuck tightly together (except one I shall discuss next) in town and around campus. I never saw any fewer than five of them together in downtown Fredericton.

They told me they felt endangered in New Brunswick. Their closing ranks wherever they went was their way of trying to forestall any tragedy that might befall them. As M'njaria put it, "Dr. Heath, there are too many crackers around here, many more crackers than you can buy in all the grocery stores in New Brunswick combined!"

One of the twelve Kenyans, Sudi, was a Sikh whose turbaned head, full-bearded face, and wire-frame glasses stood out prominently among the throng of 52 in Comparative Education. Sudi looked at least forty to me, behind that beard, but I learned from him near the end of summer session that he was only twenty-three.

Sudi proved a great asset to me as I lectured on the impact of Eastern philosophies on European and North American student protest. He had lived with the philosophies that I had but studied. So I leaned on Sudi for reassurance in a zone that was shaky territory for me. He registered his approval of my assertions in my lectures with small smiles, dips of his turban, and brown eyes that shined agreement. It was reassuring to know that I could make the inscrutable Eastern philosophies clear so that even an insider such as Sudi would attest to the clarity of my lectures.

One morning, Sudi brought a wood-and-metal prayer wheel to class to hold fervently, his eyes tightly closed as he prayed and drank in what I had to say. I must confess that this was a big ego trip for me.

At the end of class, Sudi approached the auditorium stage from where I lectured, piously carrying his prayer wheel on his palms. I leaned forward to hear what profound observation he had to make. "Do you like it?" he asked.

"Oh yes indeed. It's beautiful."

"I'm proud of it."

"You must chant many wonderful mantras with it."

Sudi looked puzzled at first, then he smiled. "Oh no sir. You have a misunderstanding in your mind. This is the napkin holder I made in technology class. Everyone says it is beautiful, that my work is very excellent, and you agree, sir. This makes me happy."

Later, Sudi came to my office to speak confidentially just prior to the final exam. "I hope you can, sir, remember," he said in a thin, meek voice, "that I know little about this kind of class when you grade my test. I am a trade-school graduate. My specialty is making objects in wood, metal, and glass, not the stuff you do."

The Dean of the University of New Brunswick Faculty of Education was forty-year-old Dr. Don A. MacIver, a tall, bearded, off-the-wall kind of guy, an animated conversationalist with a great sense of humor. Beneath a toilet seat on the wall of his office appeared the message, "All Complaints Go Here." His Scottish accent was pleasant music for me to hear from this man who had emigrated from Scotland and made good in Canada. He dressed casually, and his russet hair was longish, which contributed to the openness and informality that were his trademarks. Don was simply the most laid-back and genuine administrator I had ever worked for.

One evening Don and his British wife gave a wine and cheese party in their home in downtown Fredericton. The event brought together the summer school faculty for a couple hours of convivial gab and fine food and drink. Mrs. MacIver had put the event together and she socialized affably among us as hostess, as did Don, as host. I left their Victorian-style home -- that had recently been meticulously refurbished -- full of good feelings toward everything and anyone connected with the university and the town.

Dr. MacIver had recently been to Kenya on behalf of CIDA and the University. He had become gravely ill with hepatitis C and he was just recovering from "being white as a sheet," as he put it through a big smile. (He was a congenital smiler. I never saw him without one, or at least the hint of one.)

I observed that the Kenyans in my class liked MacIver. I think it was because of his animation, his ebullience, his constant expressiveness, especially those wonderful smiles, which communicated over the limited school English most of them commanded. (Wanami was the exception. In fact, Wanami could be downright eloquent in his second language, English.) I noted that the Kenyans didn't warm at all to those with staid personalities who could not put them at ease and communicate non-verbally with expressions and gesticulations. And oh how that Scotsman MacIver could gesticulate! Indeed, Don had it

115

made with them. He was a natural for representing the University and CIDA.

Don MacIver was a true Canadian immigrant success story. Effectively orphaned at age one (He hadn't seen his parents since.), he eventually emigrated from Scotland to Canada where he became a policeman, then a teacher, as he worked his way through a doctoral program at the University of Alberta. He did it all himself. No one helped him. A former colleague of Don's, Dr. Raj Pannu, told me during an interview at the University of Alberta in July, 1976, "Don is proud of what he's accomplished. He's done it all himself...He couldn't come here this summer to teach a short course we'd scheduled for him, as his parents, whom he's never really gotten to know, are gravely ill. One is in England. The other lives in Australia. He wants to visit them before they die." A true success story, I think, one that tugs at the heart strings, of a self-made man who overcame. It was a special privilege to get to know him.

On staff with me at the University of New Brunswick was a man I'll call "Toff," who was teaching a couple summer courses in his field. Toff became a summertime grass bachelor because his wife had refused to accompany him to Fredericton. "I like my kids, but not my wife," he told me. "If I had it all over again to do, I'd never get married, not with all the new sexual freedom we have in Canada now...My wife's Japanese, but she's been Canadianized, so she's gone completely to seed as a wife. She's no longer worth a damn...I met her in Japan, so I didn't know better. I was fooled. I didn't think she'd become a completely Canadian woman in no less than five years. Worse than most Canadian women even! Hell, when I was over there, it was so nice to be with her. In Japan they have the relations between the sexes right. The man is master, and the woman doesn't challenge it. A woman who is too forward, too aggressive, over there is not regarded too highly...When a man at the dinner table is through with one plate over there, the woman whisks it away and another takes its place." Toff shrugged and sighed heavily, wistfully. "I tell you, Gary, in Canada it's so much more difficult to be a man these days. The women walk all over you."

Toff spent his entire summer "chasing ass," as he put it. At least he told some pretty tall stories, full of detail, about chasing ass. I suspect most of what he said was pure fiction, wishful thinking spilled out into wishful anecdotes.

The tallest story Toff told me may have contained some truth. He told it to me one evening over drinks at the Lord Beaverbrook cocktail lounge. It was about his first sexual experience, which I recorded as close to **verbatim** as I could in my diary later the same night. **Excerpts:** "I was eleven years old and we met in the barn on a Sunday afternoon. It was my first experience with a woman, and I was especially nervous because she was five years older than me...We did it on a pile of blankets we spread on the hay...She bled all over the blankets and I got sick and vomited all over her."

Of his extramarital affairs, Toff boasted, "This secretary I know called me, and said, 'My husband is out of town this weekend, and I'm tight and horny.'...We met at my office downtown and had sex on a sleeping bag I spread onto the carpet...Usually on Sunday, no one is around, but goddam if someone didn't come in that Sunday, when we're hot and heavy into it. I just managed to pull out of her and get up in enough time to close the office door before he turned the corner and got into my hallway. It was the guy who has the office next to mine, damn his hide. I just got the door closed in the nick of time and the lights switched off, and cooled down enough, both of us, to avoid some very embarrassing detection. It would have been a bad scene for me on the job if that guy had seen us and let the word slip what we were doing. He would've too. He's no friend of mine...I've done it with women in my office on Sundays many times and that's the closest I ever came to having any problems."

On Dominion Day, Professor Russell A. McNeilly invited me to his home at 428 Pederson Crescent in Fredericton for a holiday picnic. We were blessed with a clear, balmy day. Russell, his Scottish-born wife, and I sat on lawn chairs in the yard, talking and drinking iced tea. The McNeillys impressed me as a particularly happy couple. Their two-year-old daughter romped on the lawn, a delightful, expressive child, full of pure energy that would not wane even under the full sun. Mrs. McNeilly was six months' pregnant with their second child. She and Russell were joyously looking forward to expanding their family, to having a sibling for the two-year-old.

Russell had joined the UNB Faculty of Education nine years before, in 1966, qualified by his M.A. from McGill and his LCP from the University of London. He taught educational statistics.

He too was an immigrant Canadian, from the Caribbean. He spoke with a soft, lilting accent that enchanted and soothed. On my visit to his home for a barbecue picnic, he and his wife were most cordial hosts. As I took my leave of them, I felt I had just spent time in the presence of family, so well did we connect with each other, airing our views, venting our frustrations, and in compelling other ways sharing our lives as we ate New Brunswick crab smoked over a grill.

Dr. Tom Gleason, visiting professor from Memorial University of Newfoundland, and I played tennis regularly on campus courts. Although Tom was twenty years older than me, I had trouble beating him. In fact, often he won. He was in fantastic shape for a fifty-year-old who had recently undergone an hemorrhoidectomy.

Tom, I, and Dr. Cal Schlick, another visiting summer prof, a superintendent of curriculum and instructional services for the Mamaroneck Public Schools in New York, took a weekend car tour of eastern New Brunswick, stopping at Mount Allison University in Sackville, where Tom had been a faculty member before taking his Newfoundland Memorial position. The small campus of lovely red sandstone buildings offered ponds, gardens, and crisscrossing walkways through bowers of elm, ash, and maple. The small town of Sackville, located on the edge of the Tantramar Marshlands, largely drained to produce wide vistas of lush hayfields, is located not far from the Bay of Fundy. I was so charmed by the campus and the town that I applied a few months later to teach summer school there. (Result: Dear Dr. Heath, I must apologize that your letter of February 2, 1976 somehow did not get answered. Let me say that your inquiry is much appreciated but the summer school vacancies were all filled before Christmas. With regrets. Yours sincerely, Gerald T. Rimmington, Professor and Head, Department of Education.)

Tom pointed out the women's residence, Harper Hall, and remarked, "That's where the men went streaking recently. The numbskulls went in there with nothing on but galoshes and raincoats one night, doffed them in the lobby, and ran naked through the hall. But the women weren't going to reward that insanity by going into shock. They hid the men's rain gear, and they had to go home naked, in the middle of the night, with the rain pouring down, and a brisk, chill wind sweeping in off the Bay of Fundy that whistled frigidly over their penises and up their cracks."

After a couple hours in Sackville, we drove to the farm of Acadian apple grower Louis Bourgeois, near the village of Pré D'en Haut-Belliveau in Westmoreland County. Tom had also been a prof at the Université de Moncton in nearby Moncton prior to his appointment in Newfoundland. He and his wife, Marie, a writer, had rented a small house from Bourgeois which stood about fifty yards from Louis' own home. Louis and Tom had become good friends during his two-year tenancy. "The tenant I have now," confided Louis, "is nowhere as good as Tom was. He doesn't keep a nice garden like Tom did either."

Louis gave us a tour of his apple orchards, pointing out where "a gang of motorcyclists" had cut over his property, and the huge storage building where a sizable portion of his crop each year was kept fresh with a special gas under pressure in low-temperature lockers throughout the months following the harvest so that the apples could be sold at times throughout the year when they brought the best prices.

Louis told me that he relied heavily on research reports from institutions like Michigan State University for insect and disease control and other aspects of crop management, to help make a success of his orchards, which, lying in far eastern New Brunswick, are on the northern fringe of the broad zone where apples are commercially feasible.

We had arrived unannounced shortly after the Bourgeois family had finished their afternoon meal in their fine, spacious home overlooking a beautiful lake. Since Mrs. Bourgeois was busy helping her daughter get ready for a big Friday night date, Louis drove us into Pré D'en Haut-Belliveau and bought us an order of takeout food (hot beef sandwiches and potato salad). On the way back, he pointed out decaying dikes constructed of spruce and pine logs that had been built by his Acadian ancestors over a hundred years before and which had long since been replaced by modern, steel-and-concrete means of water control located elsewhere. By the time we'd returned to the house, Mrs. Bourgeois had had enough time to prepare a thick soup made from fresh vegetables to accompany our sandwiches and salad.

The beautiful Bourgeois daughter looked as good as any Miss Canada to me, with her soft, flowing, dark hair and bright smile. She was clad in a perfect size-7 bright red dress that fit her lithe, youthful figure perfectly. The young woman of sixteen came across as being very feminine. "We raise our girls to be women here," said Mrs. Bourgeois. Soon a handsome, strapping young man, about seventeen or eighteen, appeared at the screen door to pick up the daughter for their evening of entertainment in Moncton. As they drove down the gravel access road to the farm in his high-gloss blue Chevrolet, my opinion of rural life in the Maritimes ratcheted upward.

Louis Bourgeois ran a substantial business operation on his sprawling apple farm of eighty acres. He is a good farmer and businessman, well versed in many facets of horticulture and marketing. Though he had never taken a college course, he was considerably self-educated, and, very impressively, he was perfectly bilingual, moving back and forth between French (which he spoke to several in the brasserie in the village when we picked up our food) and English, which he spoke with ease to us.

It galled Louis that his relatives, such as his brother who dropped in for a few minutes while we were there, thought he was rich. That was far from the truth. Though his farm is sizable, his overhead and capital investment are great, and his crop, grown in a short, frost-risky season, had to compete with British Columbia apples, which were more easily grown in the more moderate B. C. climate. What Louis got for his long hard hours, large investment, broad knowledge, anxious moments, and business acumen boiled down to a modest income.

We stayed overnight in Louis' home and in the morning were served a hearty, farm-style breakfast of coffee, orange juice, milk, toast, hot cereal, scrambled eggs, sizzling hot links of sausage, succulent bacon, and steaming thick slices of ham. Mrs. Bourgeois loaded the kitchen table till it creaked from the weight of the breakfast she had prepared. It was a true trencherman's breakfast, a compensation for the fact that she could not cook dinner for us the night before, I thought, and a pleasantly fortifying way to send us off on our return drive to Fredericton that warm, azure Sunday morning.

That summer, an inmate killed a prison guard in Ontario. The Fredericton newspaper, **The Daily Gleaner**, "The Voice of Central New Brunswick," published a good number of letters about the tragedy, most of them calling shrilly for the death penalty. Not one expressed a smidgeon of concern for the murdered guard's wife and kids or a desire to prevent future killings of guards. Revenge was all that mattered.

The Daily Gleaner published bloodcurdling editorials that reinforced the bloodlust expressed in the letters to the editor. I

G. Louis Heath, Ph.D.

had been reading this newspaper throughout the summer, and the tribalism that was vented over the killing of the guard prompted me to write a bit of doggerel:

The Daily Gleaner

We print all the news that's fit to tell
Gossip, accidents, that's what we sell.
Also editorials, letters, and crime.
A lot for a nickel and a dime.
The budworm's eating our trees?
We'll cover that, whatever you please!
The mackerel fishermen are on strike?
We'll do that, whatever you like!
Fellow Frederictonians, we certainly try
To get out a paper you'll wanna buy.
But please remember, we ain't great literature.
We know our words won't endure.
So each evening, read your **Gleaner**,
And wrap scraps in it to make things cleaner!

My summer in New Brunswick, I watched with great interest the Canadian TV coverage of Lieutenant General Van Quang, South Vietnam's former secret police director who had departed a refugee camp in Arkansas to join his wife and children in Montreal in May, 1975. The pudgy general and his family stayed at the Notre-Dame-de-Grace residence of Nguyen Tan Doi, the South Vietnamese banker who had embezzled $10 million from his country's second largest bank.

General Quang immediately became a controversial figure. After the media reported how corrupt he was, he became a huge embarrassment to the Canadian government. The newspapers reported that he had served as corps commander in the Mekong Delta until American complaints about his dishonesty had compelled South Vietnamese President Nguyen Van Thieu to transfer him to the post of "special adviser on security and national defense," where he earned a reputation for behind-locked-doors, police-state tactics and skimmed a fortune off narcotics traffic.

A TV cameraman had managed to film Quang as he walked briskly from Nguyen Tan Doi's palatial home to a waiting limousine, wearing sunglasses and shielding the lower part of his face with the collar of his jacket. The anchor reporting the film clip intoned, "General Quang would not reply to questions. However, we do know that he is here on a temporary visa and intends to apply for landed immigrant status, as his wife and children already have done...Yet, public opinion is mounting against the general and his family remaining in Canada...The House of Commons has begun to discuss the possibility of deporting him."

I yelled at the TV set, "For chrisesake, deport the damn crook! Let his people get their hands on him! It's for assholes like him that a lot of American men died!" I paused, tears coming to my eyes. "And deport that damn crook banker Nguyen Tan Doi, too! Get 'em out of Canada! They're both Un-Canadian as hell!"

I hurled my empty, styrofoam coffee cup at the TV. That gesture helped me release a little of the huge tension that remained in me, a tension that had built ever since the war began and had dissipated very little even though the war had ended two months earlier with official U.S. withdrawal.

Despite public resistance to Quang's presence, by the time I left New Brunswick in late August, Immigration Minister Robert Andras had not acted to cancel the general's special, one-year, temporary visa.

A good number of excellent term papers were submitted in my UNB classes. Three of the best were:

Corwin T. Hall, "A Review of the New Brunswick French-speaking Teacher's Association's Support of Québec's Bill 22," 16 pages.

Hall drew on several sources to look at the position of AEFNB (L'Association des Enseignants Francophones du Nouveau Brunswick) that argued that Québec's Bill 22, limiting the parents' right to choose the language of education for their child, did not conflict with New Brunswick's Official Languages Act, which stipulates that "when English is the maternal tongue of students, English must be the principal language of teaching." The administrative council of the association asserted that Bill 22 would adequately protect the linguistic rights of the Anglophone minority in Québec and would guarantee it an education in the English language.

"The AEFNB approves of Bill 22's section pertaining to education," wrote Hall, "and feels it could be dangerous to allow parents to select the language of instruction for their children without regard to the student's maternal language. It feels this would justify the admission of Anglophone students into French classes, a move the AEFNB has strenuously opposed all along." The AEFNB feared that if such permission were given, English parents would volunteer to send their children to French schools to make them bilingual, producing a problem for the French in that the English kids in their schools would soon engender an English-speaking environment, defeating the aims of both groups.

Hall concluded his paper by criticizing the sections of Bill 22 which require parents who are neither Francophone nor Anglophone -- Portuguese, for example -- to have their children educated in French.

Ed O'Coughlin, "The New Brunswick Teachers Federation's New Contract Agreement With the Provincial Government," 19 pages.

Synopsis: This paper discussed the teachers' grievances that produced a threatened strike and a work-to-rule campaign. The final agreement gave New Brunswick's 8,000 teachers much of what they had wanted: a 44% salary increase over two years -- January 1, 1975 to December 31, 1976 -- to bring their badly lagging salaries into line with those of teachers in other provinces, and a reduction of class size from 39 to 37. Provincial Education Minister Gerald Merrithew and teacher union president Paul Bourgeois did the bulk of the negotiating to reach the agreement.

Kerry B. Truman, "The Indian Women of the Caughnawaga Reserve, Québec," 15 pages, two maps.

Synopsis: This paper reported on the Québec government's request of the federal government to halt the eviction of sixty Indian women and their families from the Caughnawaga Reserve. The 101-year-old Indian Act denies Indian women who marry non-Indians the right to live, own property, or be buried on reserves. (Indian men who marry non-Indians retain these rights and pass them on to their children.) Accordingly, in late June, 1975, just before my classes at UNB began, Caughnawaga Chief Ronald Kirby ordered the women and their families off the reserve. The women and about 240 children were given till September 1 to leave, after which date they would face eviction.

Truman concluded that the Indian Act should be amended to grant women the same rights as men.

Summer Expenses

Gas. I paid an average of 77.9 cents per Canadian gallon of regular that summer. At Clancy's Gas Bar in Kingston, Ontario, I ponied up $3.05 for four gallons. Pearce and Bréault Motors in Tilbury, Ontario charged me $5.03 for 6.3 gallons. Lac St. Francois Auto, St. Zotique, Québec, pumped 5.5 gallons for $4.75, and the Shell Gas Bar of Cacouna, P.Q., charged $6.02 for 7.7 gallons. Lucien Bédard Shell, in beautiful Ste. Foy, Québec, sold me 5.9 gallons for $4.70. And throughout the summer, in

G. Louis Heath, Ph.D.

stately Fredericton, the Irving Oil station at 1169 Regent Street, which I patronized regularly, charged me 81.9 cents for regular.

How much did the University of New Brunswick reimburse me for round-trip mileage from Normal, Illinois to Fredericton? Answer: $274.

Room Rents. A room in the Hotel Waterloo in depressing, downtown Waterloo, Ontario ("Erin Barnes, clerk") cost me $7.50. The Plaza Hotel in alluring Kingston, Ontario overlooking the wind-whipped Bay of Quinte billed me $10.50 for lodging ("B. Allure, clerk"). Chambre No. 62 in the Chateau Grandville Hotel ("Sous la direction de Mailloux & Fils Ltée") in tumescent Riviere-du-Loup, with its penchant for painting church spires silver, was priced at $13. The Grandville was an especially charming hotel, old but very clean, and located smack-dab in the historic downtown. The oak wainscoting and ceiling beams gleamed with recent varnish and the refurbished, manually-operated cage elevators worked like a charm. My only complaint was that the clerk tried to get away with overcharging me, pretending he didn't know a word of English when I went about setting the matter straight.

My summer session room at the University of New Brunswick from July 1st to August 9th -- number 309 Aitken -- ran me $250. It was a fine double room that I occupied alone, as did others in Aitken, because of the greatly reduced enrollment in UNB's summer session in recent years.

Movies. I paid $2.50 to see movies at the Plaza Cinema ("A Famous Players Theatre") till July 15 when the price went to $2.75.

On August 1st, a powerful earthquake registering 6.1 on the Richter scale hit Oroville, California where my parents lived. Tremor after tremor shook the area, threatening to burst the world's largest earth-filled dam, six miles up the Feather River from downtown. That calamity would have flooded Oroville.

As soon as I heard the news, I phoned my father. He reported, "We have ripples and little explosions of whitewater ruffling the surface of our swimming pool all the time. The tremors are running through the ground all the time, though the worst seems to be over...We have some cracked windows and stuff that flew all over the place inside, but the house is still on its foundation...Mom, she's out at the Feather River Shopping Plaza right now, though she's very frightened...You know how she worried about water and couldn't sleep well for so long after we got flooded out of the old home place in 1955, when so many people died in Yuba City, and the old place collapsed into that Chinese gold-mining tunnel that ran under the house. What a shock that was. Remember how you, Mother, and Larry had to stay with your Aunt?"

"I sure do remember. I was only eleven, but I remember it all. Do you see the irony now? The Oroville Dam was built to prevent a repeat of the 1955 flood, and it has, several times. But if a quake should break her open, it would produce the worst flood ever. Oroville would be wiped out with one big squeegee action by the world's largest earth-filled dam!"

"We would all go down the drain very quickly," agreed Dad. "It looks like she's holding though, this time. Thank God she's holding." He abruptly changed the subject. "How are things in Fredericton?" he asked.

"Good, very good, a nice place to teach up here. I'm having a great summer!"

127

Chapter 5

University of Regina, 1976

Chronology: Regina College was founded in **1911** by the Methodist Church. In **1934**, the Church transferred title to the College to the University of Saskatchewan. In **1959**, Regina College became a bachelor's degree-granting institution and the second campus of the University of Saskatchewan. On **July 1, 1974**, Regina College was renamed the University of Regina and given full autonomy. On **July 31, 1976**, Dr. G. Louis Heath arrived on campus to teach a three-week course, Sociology of Education.

Bill Cheers, a thirtyish barrel of a man with a head of longish, jet-black hair, sat near the back of my class. He was a talkative, exuberant person, conversant with contemporary, ethical and social issues.

I regularly acknowledged his uplifted arm. He always had something worthwhile to say.

Bill stopped by my office several times after class to talk of the plight of the Canadian Indians whose problems he had come to know well as a teacher at an Indian reserve school. "On Treaty Day in July," he told me, "the entire reserve goes on a binge. Everybody puts some of their treaty money into the pot and they rent a truck and go down to Battleford and fill it up with booze, a great variety of it to satisfy every taste. They tend to buy cheaper stuff so they can stay drunk longer."

"When the truck gets back to the reserve, it's drink, drink, drink, all day, and all night too, if they don't pass out first...Of course, some Indians aren't drinkers, but most are, and a lot of those are out-and-out alcoholics. Different sources give different figures on their rates of alcoholism, but suffice it to say all the reserves are rife with it...The binge lasts a month or so. It's over when the treaty money is gone, and they go back to depending exclusively on welfare...During that month, a few Cree die who wouldn't otherwise. Auto accidents under the influence. Fights under the influence. Falling into a lake or river, or falling from a high place, all under the influence."

"It sounds very bad," I observed, "to be reduced to that."

"It is sad for sure, eh, and even sadder because the reserve Indians were once successful farmers in southern Saskatchewan and Alberta in the 1800s. But the whites passed some laws so they could take their land. And then they made it illegal for the Indians to sell crops in competition with the whites...The Indians were gradually demoralized. There was no way for them to work hard and get ahead. If they accumulated something, the whites would find a way to grab it. So, they lost their drive, and sank into apathy, and began to drink heavily...Eventually, the whites moved the Cree and other Indians out of the fertile agricultural zone entirely, up into the muskeg, tamarack, and rocks where the reserves are now, where commercially viable farming is impossible. Those Indians up there, I tell you, Dr. Heath, over the past one hundred years, they were destroyed. They have been completely dispirited because opportunity has been blocked to them at every juncture."

The more I listened to Bill, the more I realized what a valuable teacher he must have been during his years among the Indians. "You are a rare one, Bill," I said. "Very few idealists like you are able to survive in the schools the Indians attend. The insensitive school bureaucracy, the prejudice of the surrounding community, the horrendous problems the kids bring, the whole schmear, they conspire to drive out the idealist who wants to help."

Bill gave me a sad look. "Don't kid yourself, Dr. Heath. I got driven out, just like the rest. The only difference is that I lasted four years. Most leave after the first year. I had to leave. The strain, financially and emotionally, did me in. The whole schmear, as you put it, got to me, and I also needed to make more money to support my family and finish my degree. I left

129

teaching to drive a soft-drink delivery truck, which paid twice what I made teaching. I had to have that extra income to provide for my family."

Bill invited me to his home at 2325-29th Avenue on a Saturday night to meet his family and have a snack and a couple beers. He picked me up on campus at seven p.m.

He, his wife Karen, and I talked lengthily. Eventually we got onto Saskatchewan politics and especially the Commonwealth Co-operative Confederation (CCF) that was the precursor of the New Democratic Party. Gordon noted that the CCF, founded in Calgary in 1932, convened its first national convention in Regina in July of 1933. At that convention, the delegates wrote a party platform and a constitution. "They called that platform the 'Regina Manifesto'," Bill said. "It's famous in Canada. It called for a planned economy to eliminate poverty, unemployment, excess profits, and exploitation of the consumer and worker." Bill took a swig of his beer as his eyes took on a supremely nostalgic cast, an accomplishment for a 35-year-old man, born well after 1933. "They called those tough years the Dirty Thirties," he said in a wistful tone. "It was really poor here then. People were desperate. The really poor were lucky to get enough food. Almost everyone was just eking out an existence...But the CCF and their Regina Manifesto helped change that. They worked for unemployment insurance and lobbied the government to provide jobs, and in 1935, Prime Minister Robert Bennett, of the Conservative Party, introduced legislation a bit similar to your New Deal under Roosevelt. But Bennett didn't do enough. He did only what the people absolutely insisted on. Much more had to be done after he was voted out later the same year."

"Progress really took hold after that reactionary asshole was deposed. But, for sure, something had to be done in '35 by whoever was in power. People were rioting, including here in Regina. Some were injured. Some were killed. Dramatic change was clearly overdue!"

Our long evening's conversation also ranged over John D. Diefenbaker, the former Prime Minister of Canada who hailed from Saskatchewan; the police strike in Regina the month before that had brought out looters in alarmingly large numbers; and, Saskatchewan folk-rock singer Joni Mitchell who had left her native province for glitz and fame in Hollywood. She had begun her career in and around Regina and other cities across the Prairie where success playing lounges and coffee houses prompted her to move to the States to grasp for the brass ring. "She and her husband used to sing and play guitar in clubs around here," recalled Bill. "She showed great talent from the very beginning. I can see how she made it big...I can also see why she and her husband split up. It was really embarrassing the way they'd argue before an audience. They could hardly manage to contain their bickering enough to get through their performance. I guess they were simply unable to control themselves, the same way you see couples sometimes arguing on a downtown street even though people are turning to stare at them."

I had enjoyed a fine evening with Bill and his family. He drove me back to campus at one a.m. I felt very good about my visit to his home. "See you in class, Bill," I smiled, as I shut the door to his van.

I ate dinner several times in the College West Cafeteria with Tim, a 26-year-old Polish-Canadian from Winnipeg. He was in Regina the summer to take a philosophy class and brush up on his Polish prior to departing for Cracow, to do doctoral research under a Senior Citizens Foundation grant. A Ph.D. candidate in Philosophy at the University of Ottawa, his dissertation topic was the social justice philosophy of John Rawls.

Tim's father, the son of Polish immigrants, had never shown a scintilla of active interest in the Old Country. But Tim had gone gung-ho Polish. He had visited Poland twice and learned the language, irritating his father, who did not approve. "I'm doing all this on my own," said Tim. "I don't get a dime from

131

him. So he has no legitimate gripe. If he's not proud of being Polish, that's his problem. He'll have to put up with what I do."

"From what you say, Tim," I said, "apparently your father's been so busy working hard and raising eight children and becoming one hundred percent Canadian, that Poland was far down his list of priorities."

"That's it in a nutshell," returned Tim. "He has operated a dragline at a beet-processing plant for many years. He comes home exhausted each evening, with only enough energy left for dinner and a little TV and a beer."

"It's very common," I pontificated, "for the grandchildren of an immigrant couple to develop an interest in the Old Country. Research shows that they are more secure in their Canadian-ness and more at ease with the idea of being actively Polish. That's you. You're headed toward being a professor. Your father never had that luxury. He had to scrabble out a living and raise eight children. He ran scared all the way, and part of that involved running away from his Polish-ness, in order to become more fully Canadian. He had to survive and he knew that meant being as cautious, honest, hardworking, and Canadian as he could be."

Tim nodded and smiled thinly. "I know that in my gut. I learned it the hard way. I've had some hellish, brutal summer jobs in factories, working my way through the university. I'd come home aching, blistered, too tired to even eat. I'd go straight to bed, and eat hours later when I got up. So don't think I'm not capable of understanding my father." He paused meaningfully. "Nevertheless, his attitude still irritates the hell out of me."

A Canadian legal battle that summer, the case of Dr. Henry Morgentaler, greatly interested my class. Morgentaler was a physician who had performed more than 5,000 abortions in his east-end Montreal clinic. He was finally arrested for the abortion of a 26-year-old unmarried graduate student from Sierra Leone. He requested a jury trial, knowing full well that in Québec this meant facing a jury largely of Catholics, a group very opposed to abortion. But he knew from his work in his clinic that many

Québec women paid lip service to the sanctity of life in the womb, but, when it came to the semen which spurted through the lips between their legs, that if pregnancy resulted, they suddenly became more expedient than religious and sought him out for abortions. He was gambling on their real values, obscured by a hypocritical façade, in order to win acquittal.

Morgentaler's lawyers invoked the common law defense of "necessity," which recognizes that occasionally a crime must be technically committed to save a life. They also sought to shield the doctor with the Criminal Code's Section 45, which protects a physician from prosecution as long as his surgery is conducted with skill and reasonable care.

Morgentaler was acquitted.

Yet the government wasn't about to let Morgentaler wriggle off the hook through the cunning stratagem of a jury decision. In an unprecedented action, the prosecution appealed the acquittal to the Québec Court of Appeal and thence to the Supreme Court, where they convinced the judges to strictly apply Section 251 of the Criminal Code. That section prescribes that an abortion can only be performed in a hospital after a three-doctor panel has certified that the mother's life or health is in danger.

The court ruled that Morgentaler's defense was inadmissible and found him guilty as charged.

Sentenced to eighteen months in prison, Morgentaler commented on his conviction before a CTV camera just prior to checking into Bourdeau Penitentiary. "It's ludicrous," he said, "for the government to do nothing to protect women against the dangers of quack, back-alley, butcher abortion." After his statement, Dr. Morgentaler strode through the bleak, forbidding prison gates to become instantly more dangerous in stir, as a martyr and rallying point for pro-abortion forces, than he'd ever been outside.

The "Henry Morgentaler Defense Committee" soon organized protest marches. The media around the world devoted a lot of time and resources to the balding, bespectacled doctor, catapulting him to international celebrity status. And the

American Humanist Association awarded feminist Betty Friedan and Morgentaler jointly its Humanist of the Year Award, underscoring its view that women's liberation and medically safe, easily obtainable abortions are closely linked.

Wilma Chaliand did her term paper on Morgentaler. She selected the topic, she said, because Justice Minister Otto Lang, the devout Roman Catholic and father of seven who had refused to review the Morgentaler case, lived in Saskatchewan. The case thereby possessed, in her words, "hometown curiosity value."

"They shoulda never put that guy in prison!" exclaimed Wilma. "He's guilty of nothing. He's being harassed for following the dictates of his conscience."

I took a poll of the class via anonymous slips of paper. Eighteen students thought Morgentaler belonged in the penitentiary and every one of these also opposed abortion. Fifteen thought Morgentaler should have never been imprisoned, that he was innocent of any wrongdoing, especially in the larger, moral sense.

"This is really a very political case, isn't it class?" I noted, after announcing the results of my survey. "It certainly polarizes this class. I can see why Morgentaler has become the center of immense controversy. You're either for him or against him. Everyone has a view."

We had a pell-mell, heated half-hour discussion on Morgentaler. It had very little to do with the course, but someone started it and anything seemed to be grist for the mill that summer session. I called the yack-yack melee to a halt peremptorily, in order to call roll at the very end of class, before I forgot to do it at all.

After my charges had exited, I discovered that during my students' exchange of tirades, I had doodled onto my scratch pad the following:

> An egg in the hand
> Is worth two in the womb.
> Two eggs in the hand

Are worth two in the tomb.
Given today's shameful abortion rate, I'd say I'm right on.
Or maybe it's even worse? An egg in the hand is worth three in
the womb? Or four? Or five? ...

I got into a most compelling conversation with a fellow
named Clive at Fuller's Restaurant in downtown Regina. I had
never heard anything like his story before. He boggled my mind!

"Never give a party at your home when you're drunk," Clive
said thickly, the booze that he had consumed at a nearby bar still
showing its effects. "I did, and I am paying for it. Damn, am I
paying for it!" Clive took a long sip of his black coffee.

"Paying how?" I asked.

"My wife's changed," he replied, a note of distress in his
voice. "She's a lot colder toward me now. She changed after the
party."

"Lots of people give parties and get drunk," I consoled.

"Yeah, maybe, but this one was different, very different. I
had six of my buddies from work over one Saturday evening to
watch hockey on TV. We had a good time. We had quite a few
drinks and got real drunk. After the game, one of the guys asked
in jest, 'How about a little sex with your wife?' We were all
bombed by then, and so was my wife. I was so drunk the idea
seemed all right. So I said, 'Good idea. I'll go first to get the
machine warmed up for you.'

"Well, from there on out, it was an orgy. We each had my
wife once, and four guys had her twice. By then, she wasn't so
drunk and was more in control of herself. She got up, put on her
clothes, and told my friends to leave. After they left, I could tell
that she was going to make things different between us. She
hardly ever speaks to me now except to say that if it's OK for her
to have sex with six of my friends, then it's OK with her if I go
out and have six affairs."

"She sounds very resentful," I observed.

135

"Very. Our relationship has deteriorated a great deal. That's why I'm here a lot. It's too painful to be at home."

"Are your friends sorry about what's happened?"

"I don't think so. They've spread the word with the other guys at work. It's like a big dirty joke they tell. I can see them laughing among themselves and looking my way. I know what they're saying." Clive winced. "My relationship with them has changed, too. They think less of me. We are no longer friends. Unfortunately, I have to be around them because we work at the same place."

"Booze is a terrible enemy," I intoned.

Clive took another big sip of coffee. "You can say that again. Terrible. But I can't live without it now that I've lost my job and my wife's filed for divorce."

A **really** terrible enemy, I thought.

I and Rex Hawser, another visiting summer instructor, took a trip up to far northern Saskatchewan to see Rex's friend, Joe Sinclair, a man who'd fled the United States in 1967 to evade the Vietnam War draft. He had the past few years been living in the Saskatchewan wilderness, making his living off a 20-mile-long trapline. We drove on the Yellowhead Highway to North Battleford, and from there due north to Bel Butte, and far beyond to where we drove deeply rutted, primitive roads amid roiling clouds of fine, brown dust. We could hardly see out the windows as our van jolted miserably along at a snail's pace.

As an alder branch whipped across my cheek, I muttered to Rex, "Is it gonna be worth all this, Rex?"

Rex grinned. "Relax, Gary, and enjoy the pain. You have left civilization and there is no return now. This is the Saskatchewan bush. Life is tough. This is only worth it if you want to meet a rugged guy named Joe Sinclair who knows how to survive in the bush."

I leaned forward tensely, alert for the next big rut, the next big branch to go for my head, even though I had by then rolled up the window to protect myself. "I am very relaxed," I whined. "I always am when the situation is desperate."

Rex roared with laughter, enjoying my discomfort.

After six hours of crawling along, we reached a rise in the road where we stopped. After the dust had drifted away, we could see a rustic, log cabin ahead of us, snuggled in a clump of birch and aspen beside the next rise in the road not far ahead. "That's Joe's place," said Rex.

"How far did we go in those six hours since we left the asphalt?"

Rex eyed the odometer. "Twenty-one miles."

"I could've walked it quicker."

"Except the deer flies would've eaten you alive and your throat would be choked with dust."

A tall, bronzed, muscular man walked toward us. It was Joe, wearing only cut-off jeans. No shoes. Beside him lumbered a full-grown black bear. "Tame I hope?" I queried.

"Yes, very tame," replied Rex. "That's Joe's one and only family member."

"Sexually?"

"Don't be disgusting," returned Rex in a low voice as Joe reached a point but a few yards away.

"Well, it's out here in the middle of nowhere," I returned defensively.

Rex shook his head. "Not with Joe. No sodomy for him. He had a wife but she left him and took their three-year-old son with her."

"She probably didn't care for all the silly women's clubs around here," I said wryly.

Joe came to the driver's side, shook Rex's hand, and reached over and shook mine. "Joe Sinclair here," he smiled. "Nice to see you made it."

"Gary Heath here, and very pleased to be here," I said. "Does the bear have a name?"

Joe looked down and scratched the bear's head. "Golden."

"For a black bear?"

"Golden is short for Molson Golden beer. This bear always wears a necklace of Molson Golden beer caps. That's how he got his name, from the beer I drink. It's the best."

Rex got out of the van and I followed. "How long's it been, Rex?" asked Joe. "Two years?"

"Two years exactly. The last time I saw you was in August, 1974."

"You're looking good. You've lost a lot of your gut."

"I cut down on my beer drinking," laughed Rex.

Joe chuckled. "I wish I could get my hands on more beer. About the only time I can drink as much as I want is when I hike out of here for provisions and equipment." He smiled broadly, spontaneously. "By the way, did you bring those cases of Molson Golden I asked for?"

"Yessiree," replied Rex, moving toward the end of the van. "Let's take them up to your cabin while we're at it. Give a hand here, Heath."

"Yessir. I'm a-coming, I'm a-coming," I said in a mock-servile voice. Each of us carried a case toward the cabin. Golden sniffed at each case but found nothing to interest him.

Joe deftly and quickly extracted several cans from one case. "I'll be right back," he said. "I want to put these in the creek down there" -- he jabbed a finger down the hill -- "so we'll have some cool beer to drink."

The bear followed Joe while Rex and I completed the short walk to the cabin, where we deposited the cases of beer. We then made our way to the creek, to join Joe, where we washed accumulated dust off our faces and arms, took off our shoes, waded in the chill, reinvigorating water. Soon we plopped down on large granite rocks along the creek to watch Joe and Golden cavort into and about the creek. Joe splashed Golden with water and Golden returned the favor, sweeping his claws over the water and scooping a sheet of water at his master. Each time Golden splashed Joe, I could see his claws gleam in the late afternoon sunlight and I gave an inward shudder. The lethal capacity of those awesome natural tools was so evident in his frolic that it was difficult to imagine that what was going on before my eyes was play. When Joe came closer to us, and Golden began to splash Rex, then me, I yelled, "Have him stop it, Joe!" Which he did, because it was no fun for Rex and me, who were not accustomed to such reminders of our own fragility and vulnerability.

"Come here, Golden," ordered Joe sternly, and the bear obeyed immediately, bounding to him, nuzzling Joe's outstretched hand. "Don't splash Professor Heath, Golden. Your claws make him nervous. If you're nice that way, you get a beer."

"That damn bear drinks beer?" I said incredulously.

Joe ruffled the neck fur of his pet beast affectionately. "Hell, this bear was nursed on Molson Golden Beer. He doesn't know what mother's milk is. Like me, he's an alcoholic."

"Wow," I said, impressed.

Joe grinned. "This isn't an ordinary bear, y'see. This bear is half-man cuz I raised him. He's never had any bear company. The only creature he's ever known is me. If he had to go into the wilderness alone, he'd have a hard time adjusting."

"Who wouldn't?" I observed. "So far I've only taken a ride into this bush of yours and I'm already having adjustment problems, even with members of my own species around me." I pointed accusingly at Golden. "And that bear is a big adjustment problem, too. It takes some getting used to, a bear that drinks. I thought that kinda bear was for novels and movies."

Our conversation turned to Joe's erstwhile human family. "Golden's my only family now, ever since my wife left me. She couldn't take it here. She said our kid was growing up real screwed up. 'Whoever heard of a child growing up with a black bear as his only playmate,' she said. So, she split and took the kid with her."

"Where's your wife now? Did she remarry?" I asked.

139

"Remarry? We never divorced. She just walked out on me. Went back to her hometown of Red Rock, Ontario. That's a small town on the north shore of Lake Superior. She and the kid are living with her parents and she's got work as a waitress. A friend of mine wrote and told me she's dating a lot of guys, looking around a lot, saying to everyone she's single again when neither of us has even filed for divorce.

"Why I got married in the first place I'll never know. I guess I was on the rebound from losing my country when I fled the draft. I knew I couldn't go back. Maybe I was looking for something to hang onto. I dunno. It's kind of a dumb thing for someone who's not the marrying kind, to go out and get married. Just dumb." Rex and I chuckled. "Nancy's dating guys with jobs -- miners, truck drivers, guys with futures who are willing to stay put and work a job," continued Joe. "She's looking for another monkey for her leash, one that performs better," he quipped.

"You have just defined marriage," I put in sarcastically.

Joe's craggy bearded face crinkled with a smile. "I'm sure glad I took up the life of a trapper even though it ruined my marriage. I'm happy this way, with my trapline. I get every kind of animal, you name it, even some kinds I'm not supposed to. Elk, deer, weasel, moose, beaver, I get 'em. Beaver are scarce but I get my share of those, too." Joe's eyes lit up. "By the way, our beer must be cold enough to drink now." He rose, stepped into the creek, and pulled out four cans.

Joe pulled the tab for Golden's beer, and the bear bounded toward it, rising onto his hind legs, growling softly in a low key. Joe insinuated the Molson Golden between the bear's paws and withdrew his hand swiftly as Golden clamped down upon the can, and began to drink.

Golden's style of drinking was not what I expected from a bear. I expected him to drink rather quickly and violently, collapsing the can in order to squeeze out the beer. Instead, Golden proved a very fastidious tippler, taking his time, savoring every drop that he delicately slurped out of the can, allowing the brewed liquid to roll slowly down his long tongue. Perhaps he had learned that a beer was a special treat for him in the wilderness removed far from neighborhood bars and he wished to prolong the pleasure as much as possible. Or, perhaps black bears can only drink a beer by fastidiously licking at the little hole in the bottom of an upturned can.

A wed at the spectacle of a 400-pound bear drinking a beer, I asked, "Has your bear ever been drunk?"

"Once I let him drink all he wanted, about seventy cans, down in Bel Butte, and he got bombed. He broke the windows out of a few parked cars in town and killed a kid's Shetland pony. But he paid no attention to the people in the bar on his way out to wipe out the cars parked along the main street of Bel Butte."

"You mean he drank in a bar with you?" I asked in a shocked tone of voice.

"Yes indeed. When I used to work in a mill near Bel Butte, Golden had his own special stool I built for him for the Blue Royal Tavern. It was a big hit with the tavern crowd after they found out Golden wouldn't cause any trouble. A lot of people came in and drank just to see the bear drinking, perched on a huge platform of a stool beside me. They did a huge business in there cuz of Golden and after a while my bear got to do his drinking free. It was Molson Golden on the house for Golden."

"What did he do with the Shetland pony?"

"He ate it."

"Ooooh. Oh oh." I cast a worried glance at Golden.

Rex and I stayed three days with Joe, hiking a few miles up north with him, checking the trapline, and running our mouths. It was a hard three days, during which I didn't see a sign of the animals he claimed to be trapping, in or out of his traps. At the end of our arduous stay, I was very tired. I felt I had learned something though. But I couldn't put my finger on it until Joe made mention of evading the draft. "I didn't want to leave my

family in northern Michigan," he said, "but it was something I
had to do. It hurt me a lot a long time after I left home, but then I
began to mature and be proud of the action I had taken. I wasn't
going to kill any Vietnamese, to take their freedom and lives and
make a black evil thing of my own life."

Ah ha, I thought. Golden is the black metaphor for the evil
thing Joe's life could've become. It all came together for me
instantly, and I felt I had figured out his strange friendship with
the black bear. Or at least I had come up with one possible
explanation.

"Our so-called civilization drove you into the wilderness,
didn't it, Joe?"

"Gary, you have stated the obvious so well. I had to flee
society in order to avoid a beast that wants freedom and wealth
for itself but tries to deny it to others. When it began to include
me in that equation by fighting an illegal war, I got the hell out
of there. I wanted no part of us destroying a small country in the
name of freedom and democracy. At least up here, in Canada,
they don't have those kind of weird hang-ups."

"Joe, you're one of the few," observed Rex, "who can see
through the bullshit the American school system filled his mind
with. I congratulate you."

Joe took a quaff of beer. "My family taught me some human
values and the ability to think critically that the schools refuse to
teach. I could see through the bullshit. I could see that a high
school principal in my former country is no better than a high
school principal in Nazi Germany. They aren't educated at all,
and they do anything they're told, anything at all. And the same
for the students. How else could Vietnam have happened?"

I disagreed with Joe's assessment -- I knew many fine,
highly idealistic principals in Illinois schools through my job in
the Illinois State University College of Education -- but I did
not challenge him. Instead, I chimed in about the complicity of
higher education. "And I might add," I said, "that professors at
top universities, Berkeley, Harvard, Columbia, some of them
will say anything that power and money dictate, fitting into the

system you saw in the schools of Michigan. Truth becomes power and money for some professors."

"It gets worse higher up?"

I nodded glumly. "Indeed it does."

"I'm glad I never thought seriously about going to college," concluded Joe.

"It wouldn't have done you any good at all," I observed, looking about me at the ramshackle cabin surrounded by spindly birch and spongy, boundless muskeg, "given the price you are willing to pay to do your own thinking."

Summer Expenses

Gas. I paid an average of 76.9 cents per Canadian gallon of regular. For 5.9 gallons at Albert Park Service Centre in Regina, I paid $4.50, and for 7.2 gallons at Hillsdale Twin Service, also in Regina, I coughed up $5.55. $5.59 for 6.4 gallons at Battleford's Esso Service in North Battleford, Saskatchewan ("TIRES – BATTERIES –ACCESSORIES – LUBRICATION – TUNE UPS – BRAKE JOBS – AAA EMERGENCY TOWING"). Etcetera.

My mileage for the summer figured at 26.2 miles per gallon in my 1969 Volkswagen. My Illinois license plate number for 1976 was CE 8418. And on July 29, 1976, my odometer read 85,214 miles. That was the day I bought a 560x15 tire for $25.15 at the Firestone store in downtown Regina.

So much for my car log, except to say that a quart of Shell X-100 cost me $1.55 at the Albert Park Service Centre in Regina, the station I frequented most during my summer session course.

Rooms. I paid $4 for one night in Saskatchewan Hall at the University of Saskatchewan in Saskatoon. (I have yet to return their towel. It has wiped a lot of residual snow off my car in Illinois and lately, Iowa.) I paid $95 for bed-sitting room S-3-1 in College West Residence at the University of Regina for August 1 through 29.

Movies. Admission to the Roxy Theatre and the Famous Players Theatres, the Metropolitan and the Broadway, in Regina, was $3.25. I saw six movies, mostly to escape my stuffy room in College West Residence, not because I thought John Wayne in "The Shootist" was especially good.

Regina offered, in addition to "The Shootist," the following silver-screen fare during the three weeks of my sojourn: Raquel Welch, Bill Cosby, and Harvey Keitel in "Mother Jugs & Speed;" Robert Redford, Faye Dunaway, Cliff Robertson, and Max Von Sydow in "Three Days of the Condor;" Jack Nicholson in "One Flew Over The Cuckoo's Nest;" and, Walter Matthau and Tatum O'Neal in "The Bad News Bears." Unfortunately, I found no Canadian movies to go see, though I was dying to see some.

Groceries. I ate most my meals in the College West cafeteria and at Fuller's Restaurant downtown, but I cooked enough in the communal kitchen to become aware of grocery prices. For example: Gainers Capital Side Bacon, one-pound package, $1.59; Frying Breasts, Chicken, Tray Pack, $1.19 a pound; and, Burns Pride of Canada Wieners, one-pound package, 89 cents.

One afternoon, as I stood at the stove boiling a couple of Burns Wieners, I responded to a knock at the door. "Annual inspection," droned a young woman clad in jeans and plaid blouse who looked like a student. "How are the five of you doing in here?" she asked perfunctorily, glancing down at a pad on her clipboard.

"We get by," I said.

"Good," she said. "Excellent really. I'll write down 'excellent' for you all. You don't want to just get by. Always go for more. Be number one." She then walked briskly on her way.

I felt the five of us with bed-sitting rooms in our suite were quite fortunate to have gotten through the annual inspection. With no one taking much responsibility for anything except his own cache of food in the fridge, the kitchen had become a study in varicolored food stains and spills, and the living room sofa and carpet had taken on a redolent life of their own. It was certainly lucky she didn't actually inspect us!

I finish the summer expenses segment with my letter of appointment and salary (that paid the above expenses), sent to me on May 28, 1976 at Illinois State University:

I am pleased to advise you officially of your appointment to teach Sociology of Education E305 in Session E of the University of Regina Summer Session August 3 to August 27, 1976.

The stipend is $1,560.00.

As a visiting instructor you are entitled to a living allowance of $100 and a travel allowance of the equivalent to return economy air fare from your place of residence to Regina, to a maximum of $350.00.

Government regulations and those of the University require that you complete certain documents upon arrival at the University of Regina. To do this, would you kindly call at the Personnel Office, 206 Administration-Humanities Bldg.

I would be grateful for a brief note confirming your acceptance of this appointment.

Enclosed is an Instructor's Guide which has been prepared to provide instructors with information about various procedures and practices during the Spring and Summer Sessions. The last page of this guide must be completed before your stipend can be paid.

Sincerely,

H.G. Kindred
Director of Extension

Two term papers in my class of seventeen earned a top grade of 19 from me on the University of Regina scale of 20. They were:

Elaine Marger, "Indian Control of Education," 29 pages. This paper discussed the detailed recommendations contained in the Canadian National Indian Brotherhood's December 12, 1972 policy paper, "Indian Control of Education" (Ottawa: Mail-O-Matic Printing, 1972).

Marger explained her interest in the topic. "I teach in an integrated, Indian-white school at Raymore, Saskatchewan, which is in the Govan Unit. We have had Indians attending the school from the Poorman Reserve for 15 years. In that time we have had two native students graduate from Grade 12...I often feel inadequate in teaching these youngsters and would like to know more about them...Another reason I chose the topic was because the Saskatchewan representative on the committee which produced the policy paper was Rodney Soonias who spoke at two intercultural conferences held in our area. He is a very dynamic and impressive speaker. He really believes in the Indian cause. At one point in his teens, he was so frustrated that he contemplated suicide. However, he did not fire the gun. Instead, he went on and got his Master's degree in Education and is now doing a great deal to help the Indian cause."

Margaret Hjelte, "The Decline of Prairie Towns," 19 pages. Hjelte reviewed Lloyd H. Person's **Growing Up In Minby** (Western Producer Prairie Books, 1976).

"Minby" is Swedish for "my town," a term Dr. Person uses to designate the composite of Craik and Aylesbury, Saskatchewan, where he grew up in the late 1920s and early '30s. It was the Minby to which his Swedish immigrant parents came in 1903. They opened a blacksmith shop in Minby and it was from Minby that Lloyd Person left for military service in World War II. He returned to Saskatchewan for university study, later becoming a professor at the University of Regina.

Hjelte explained her interest in the book. "I was raised in a prairie town and enjoyed some of the same heart-warming experiences. The town where I was raised, Chamberlain,

146

Saskatchewan, like my parents before me, is next to Aylesbury and is often mentioned in his book. Person's description of the town and its people are very comparable to the people my mother talks about in Chamberlain."

Professor J. Orrison Burgess and his wife Rosemarie invited about twenty university people, including me, to a party at their home at 2626 Albert Street at 5 p.m. on Wednesday, August 11th. We had shish kebab, potato salad, chips and dip, beer and cola. Rosemarie had prepared the beef in a special, secret-recipe marinade and Orrison did the cooking on a barbecue grill on the backyard patio. Everyone took their chunks of meat and vegetables straight off the grill, according to the way they wished them done. I loaded two skewers with grilled beef, potato, onion, and mushroom. The marinade, I thought, made the shish kebab, and this marinade was even better than that I had enjoyed at Professor Russ McNeilly's the previous summer in Fredericton, New Brunswick.

At the party, I got to talk with some highly interesting people, including the Burgesses. I learned they had spent a year in Lagos, Nigeria with the Canadian International Development Agency. "We were regarded as Americans while we were in Africa," Rosemarie noted archly in a near-accusatory voice. "We didn't like that one bit."

Orrison showed me his Nigerian wood carvings in the living room, including Ibo and Hausa masks. "Do you wear those to faculty meetings?" I asked.

Orrison eyed me dubiously and said evenly, "Never."

"You ought to try it. They'd make you look like a wild and sexy guy around campus."

"I am not interested in looking like a wild and sexy guy. I bought these masks to hang on the wall."

"I see. You're not at all interested in taking them off the wall in order to put in an off-the-wall appearance on campus, eh?"

"Never," repeated Orrison, this time in a stern voice. A tense silence held sway between us, portentously and momentously, until the Burgesses' malamute, "Adja," snuck her nose between us, begging our attention with a tongue-lolling expression.

Orrison informed, "Adja is the Yoruba word for dog."

"Naming a dog 'dog' is pretty damn dumb," I said. "Pretty damn dumb indeed. Why not the Yoruba word for powerful or fast or winter day or thick white fur?" I made a sour face. "But naming a dog 'dog,' that's so stupid it defies belief."

Orrison glowered. "I should've never told you what Adja means. Any information you get, you'll play around with and screw it up somehow, eh? I know that now. Your students say you teach that way, too. You spend a good deal of the time screwing up the material, they say."

"The time I engage students in discussion is valuable to their understanding of my lectures," I rejoined. "How come you changed your mind about my teaching? The first week I was here, you said I was doing great."

"You insulted my dog!" cried Orrison. "That did it!"

"That was the final faux pas, eh?" I glared.

Orrison turned red. "Yes, that was the final paw!" He pivoted on his heel and strode angrily away.

I also ran my mouth at the party with Don, a visiting psychology professor from the University of British Columbia. He told me about his work doing sensitivity training among Asians in the Vancouver schools. "Do you sensitize them to the fact that Canada is the most racist goddam country in the world," I challenged, playing the devil's advocate.

"I sensitize them to our social structure, our Great Canadian National Mosaic," he responded primly. "I help them to fit into our Mosaic, to polish their little tiles and get into their own little niches."

"That Mosaic concept is a lot of bull crap, y'know?" I asserted gruffly, my entire body bristling malignantly at Don.

"Our Great Canadian National Mosaic is not bull crap. It is an accurate description of who we are. I try to help the East Indians understand and appreciate that."

Fulsome, bull-crap ideology, I thought, but I challenged no more.

We went on to discuss a mutual acquaintance, Dr. Frank Engelson, with whom I had become acquainted three summers before at the University of British Columbia. "I really enjoyed knowing Frank," I observed. "We got together three or four times to run our mouths at the faculty club on Point Grey and talk sociology. He's really into soche much more in the strictly academic sense than I am. I'm more interdisciplinary and eclectic, drawing on history, philosophy, literature, anything I find useful. Frank adheres to the methodology. I guess you'd have to say he's a true sociologist."

"And a good one, too," said Don. "Did you know he's from Saskatchewan?" I shook my head. "Indeed he is...He's going through a divorce right now." Don smiled with immense self-satisfaction. "My wife would never think of leaving me. We would never divorce. She is my little sugar pussy and needs me. She couldn't make it without her Don."

"Maybe you should give your wife a little sensitivity training," I admonished. "It sounds like someone has fucked her mind up pretty bad."

Don's eyes flashed red-hot rivets at me. "Nobody fucks with my wife's mind except me!"

A retired University of Regina professor, a plump mountain of a woman with huge, flaccid mammaries, spent a half-hour at the party complaining to me about Canada. "The East Indians are taking over...The bureaucracies are insensitive...The winters are getting colder...Québec and Trudeau are ruining the country..." And so on. "I have my house up for sale," she finished. "I and the woman I share it with, we're moving to Arizona. We're getting out of here. Life is better in Arizona."

I shrugged. "Arizona is better than Canada, your own country? A single sleazy state is better than a whole big wonderful country?"

"It sure is. Have you ever been through a Regina winter?"

"Never, but I have been through some Midwestern winters."

"Well, Saskatchewan has winters ten times worse. Sixty below and you can't go outside for weeks at a time. At least you shouldn't unless you have to. It's dangerous!"

"You can have a stroke in Arizona when it hits 110 down there. It can kill you."

The woman angled her nose up snobbishly, her breasts surging toward me like a massive landslide. "We shall have air conditioning in our house," she sniffed.

I left the party about midnight. I had enjoyed myself and learned a lot, including the fact that I had made a big mistake when I had sent Orrison an autographed copy of my book, **Off The Pigs!: The History And Literature Of The Black Panther Party,** just prior to departing for Regina. Orrison told me angrily that he was a reserve commander in the Canadian Navy, and that his son was a member of the Royal Canadian Mounted Police. "Neither he nor I appreciate being offed by the likes of you or the Black Panthers," he muttered darkly.

I tried to make myself small. I skulked off into a corner, where I imagined that Orrison commanded some sort of fleet on Lake Wascana near campus, like maybe a small flotilla of resident mallards and blue-winged teal. But one thing I didn't have to imagine for sure and that was that I would never be asked back to teach at the University of Regina. I had sealed my fate on that prospect at the party!

I wonder how many careers go awry not on their own merits but because of some gaucheries committed at a party? Caught up in the festive, laid-back atmosphere, perhaps lubricated to indiscreet loquaciousness, how many aspirants for success do themselves in? They must be legion in number, intelligent and educated enough to do their jobs well, yet lacking the insight that the importance of **homo ludens** far exceeds that of **homo faber.**

Homo ludens
Homo faber
Good-bye Saskatchewan!
Good-bye!

Chapter 6

Memorial University of Newfoundland, 1977

I was hired to teach at the Grand Falls Extension Centre, in the middle of the Island, operated by Memorial University of Newfoundland the summer of 1977. On my way up to Newfoundland, I stopped two weeks in New Brunswick's largest city, St. John, a major port on the Bay of Fundy, much of it built on rocky crags overlooking the Bay. It was quite a stay, perhaps the toughest two weeks I ever spent anywhere, owing to the fact that I took a cheap, dumpy room at number 90 Mecklenburg Street, in the slummiest part of town, offering a high density of starving cats, broken glass, falling-down drunks and housing, plainclothes police, and adolescent gangs. It was the life I led in that scrofulous bailiwick that insidiously wore me down, not the city itself, most of which I found clean and attractive and offering a good deal to see and do.

My room, 1-A, lurked darkly and odiferously only five feet behind the unlockable front door to the ramshackle, two-story firetrap at 90 Mecklenburg. Twenty-four hours a day, anyone walking by could pull open that door, and see immediately across the small, curling linoleum foyer, the door to my room. The previous occupant had been a down-and-out drug addict who had beat herself silly against the walls and furniture, one bed, one dresser. She had to be hospitalized. Certainly she had left the place foul-smelling. The stains everywhere, I was told a week into my stay, were caused by her blood and vomit.

I had searched three hours for a room and 90 Mecklenburg was the only place willing to rent for only two weeks, apart from the hotels and motels, the cheapest of which was $26 a day. The room didn't at first look that bad to my naïve eyes, and what a bargain at $3 a day! What a bargain indeed! No bedding for the drug-stinking bed which drew upon my body heat to assume a life of its own, giving off a strong narcotic smell. And when I tried to get to sleep snuggled beneath a pile of clothes, I had to overcome the tinny music played by two young immigrant Pakistanis in the room above. That music, the pungent smell of spicy meals they cooked on a hot plate that mingled with the drug odor, my room's darkness (the wiring didn't deliver electricity!), the stark drabness of the room, and the frequent sound of the front door opening and closing made sleep a considerable accomplishment. When it finally came, it was my escape, and I knew what it was like to be really poor, with sleep as the only luxury.

90 Mecklenburg struck me as a warren for both the hopeless and the hopeful. The Pakistanis, Linwood Tracy, Jr. down the hall, and myself, all young and hopeful and with futures. The others, twenty or so, had no future. Old and broken, or young and on the lam, they saw the world through glasses very darkly. I imagined that the sordid, filthy hallway bathroom was for them, not for us. Its collection of bugs, cigarette butts, and sundry other forms of dirt and filth, was, to my mind, a metaphor for them.

I never used the communal bathtub, but I had to use the toilet. One morning at about five a.m., I went down the hall to use that facility and found a large teenager sleeping on the floor in front of the toilet. A knife protruded from his back pocket, the grip of a handgun beetled from his jacket, and his hands were scored with blood-dried scrapes and scratches. With alacrity, I turned on my heel and returned to my room. After ten minutes' sitting in the dark, holding a bowel movement, I realized I could not allow myself the luxury of walking away so easily from the facilities. I needed them, and soon!

I walked down the hall and rapped on Linwood Tracy's door. He was up, getting ready for work at the St. John Ironworks where he was a supervisor. He was still a little bleary-eyed. "Hey, Linwood," I said, "there is a teenaged punk sleeping in our bathroom and he's armed. Knife and gun. I don't dare go in there and wake him. He might take exception to it by carving on me or even shooting me. He looks like he's been in a fight. He's got blood on his hands."

153

Linwood, who lived at 90 Mecklenburg during the week, when he was away from his family in St. Stephen, where he owned a nice home and supported a wife and ten children (hence the need for living cheaply in St. John), accompanied me down the hall and had a look. He didn't say anything, only nodded, and returned to his room and phoned the police. "This ought to be interesting to see what happens, Gary," he smiled, returning the receiver to its cradle.

"More than interesting," I returned. "It is a compelling drama unfolding because as it unfolds it becomes increasingly compelling as my urinal pressure increases. I hope the cops get here soon!"

A stout, black woman in uniform, the only black woman on the St. John police force, arrived. "Show me your problem," she said, pulling out her handcuffs with one hand, and holding a truncheon in the other.

We led her to the bathroom, where she stepped in and prodded the young man awake. "Up fellow," she said. "Up. You're under arrest."

The punk uncurled himself and looked up. "What the fuck," he said sourly. "You woke me up!"

"I'm also arresting you on the charge of trespassing. You don't live here. For sure you can't choose to sleep in the bathroom without paying rent."

The teen peered at the woman. "I'll be a son of a bitch. A black woman cop."

She stared at the teen. "I'll be a daughter of a bitch. A white boy criminal." Then she hoisted the teen up and handcuffed him. He offered no resistance though he had the look in his eye that he would like to. "Where'd you cut your hands?" she asked. "Those are nasty cuts and bruises."

"I had to defend myself," he replied.

"You did? Why didn't you use these," she said, removing the knife and gun from his pockets.

"I like to use my fists. It makes a fairer fight."

"From the looks of your hands," she observed, "you better fight only unfair fights from now on, where you have some sort of advantage."

"I am a man!" said the teen defiantly.

"Men don't sleep with toilets," she slashed.

The fellow down the hall, balding, 39-year-old American Linwood E. Tracy, Jr. of Milltown Heights, St. Stephen, New Brunswick, a port of entry to the United States, was one of three foremen for 105 men at St. John Iron Works on Vulcan Street, overlooking the harbor. Tall, easy-going Linwood wore jeans, a cowboy hat, and boots. Others at the Iron Works called him "The Cowboy."

Linwood took me on a tour of the Iron Works, or tried to. We got about fifty feet before his three-quarter ton truck ran out of gas. It had been siphoned dry by the young hoodlums of the neighborhood. Linwood poured into his empty tank a can of gas he kept behind the seat, and that got us to a service station.

The St. John Iron Works are housed in six buildings directly behind a wharf on the harbor. They do a wide range of jobs, from manufacturing gasoline tank covers for Irving Oil to rebuilding boilers for ships and schools, to dispatching men to ships off the coast to do repairs on board, thereby saving the client the time of putting into port. The firm handles all phases of its work, including making castings in its foundry and repairing its own machines. It takes jobs others cannot even consider because it can make parts to substitute for ones no longer manufactured.

Linwood introduced me to his superior, Mr. Sanderson, a Briton about sixty, who wore a gray, pin-striped suit, glasses, and a hard hat. There was a third supervisor, in addition to Sanderson and Linwood, a Canadian. He was out on a ship doing a job. (The firm had found that supervisors of different nationalities help to draw business from a wide variety of countries, especially from those nations where the supervisors have citizenship.)

I chatted with an old fellow who worked in the rigging shop. He'd been with the Iron Works 35 years and yarned about the good old days and the great ones who had taught him his trade. After we left him, Linwood told me the man had a heart problem and hadn't recently been very productive, yet the firm was carrying him the final few months until his retirement in recognition of his years of service.

Linwood also introduced me to the company's mechanical engineer, a bronze-brown East Indian who was impeccably dressed in a fine, tan, silk suit. He was a pleasant fellow to talk with, but his apparel struck me as out of place, as his assignment was in the grimy, industrial shop, not the office where I'd met Sanderson. Later, Linwood remarked, "His fancy suits tend to isolate him from the men who work under him." Which was exactly the intent, I thought. Linwood tipped his cowboy hat at a jaunty angle and kicked out a boot. "He's the one who first started calling me The Cowboy. I call him Tonto." He let loose with a short laugh at his comment and I found myself doing the same.

We returned to the office where Linwood showed me a copy of the lengthy union contract which covered 105 employees, a good three-fourths of whom were at that very moment on ships doing repairs. "Union shop here," Linwood intoned matter-of-factly, spreading out the substantial document over his desk. "They make $8 an hour under this one."

At Elliott's Convenience Store at the corner of Duke and Charlotte Streets -- coffee 30 cents, hot dogs 19 -- I met lean, 26-year-old ex-con, Bob, who had bright-red, stubble-short hair and sported an equally stubby beard. Bob, who suffered epilepsy, had been abandoned when he was three months old and had spent his life in foster homes, juvenile halls, prisons, and rooms akin to mine on Mecklenburg Street, which were as bad as a prison. He never told me how he had happened to come to New Brunswick, but he did tell me he was a psychiatric patient, on parole, living on $155 a month from the government and "always looking for work and hardly ever finding any."

"I was shooting heroin a lot," recalled Bob, "before I got busted for car theft. That's what they put me in prison for, for stealing a car."

"Did you steal the car so you could buy drugs?"

"Right. There is a good market for auto parts, hot parts, in Montreal where I was living then. That car would've kept my habit going an entire week if I hadn't got caught." He shrugged. "But I guess it was inevitable. It was the nineteenth car I had hot-wired off a side street, and well, out in the open like that, stealing is risky.

"I was as bad a heroin addict as you can find, and that bust put me in the hospital where I had to go cold turkey before they sent me to prison. It was hell climbing out of the pit, but I was forced to it. I could've gotten drugs in prison, but I wasn't about to become some older con's lover in order to get them, and I didn't like the idea of cutting a vein open and blowing the shit right into the blood stream either. I was tempted, badly tempted, but somehow I managed to resist. After a year's cold turkey, there was no way they could tempt me. If it hadn't been for getting busted and that five months in the hospital, before they put me in the penitentiary, I'd probably be dead now. I was that bad. I was on my way to dying young."

Bob invited me to attend his T-group, conducted by a government psychologist, that evening. "It's for me and others on parole," he said. However, I could not go with him, though I liked the idea, because I had purchased a ticket to a concert that evening by a pair of Maritime folksingers who called themselves "Finnigan."

"Finnigan" -- Jim Flynn of Placentia Bay, Newfoundland and Peter Stoney of Belfast, Northern Ireland -- sang Irish and

157

Canadian songs and some of their own hilarious lyrics, including "Seven Old Ladies," "The Rock Crusher Jig," "Boogie Woogie Newfie," and "The Lobster Shuffle." They larded into their program of song short jokes such as: "Why is an Ontario brain worth $500 for a brain transplant while a Newfoundland brain is worth $1,500?" Answer: "The Newfoundland brain has never been used." And one liners: "Clap your hands, people...That's Newfoundland air conditioning."

Only about a hundred people paid $5 for the concert in the St. John High School auditorium that has a capacity of a thousand. I could see why. Flynn and Stoney were good, but for $5, a second group or a longer program should have been offered. I know I felt a little cheated when I realized that, after a mere 45 minutes, the show was over.

The City Market in downtown St. John offered spacious, colorful, clean, indoor shopping. Eggs, $1.25 a dozen. Lobster, $2.55 a pound live, $3.15 cooked. One could also buy salmon steaks, clams, and scallops. How I wished I had a kitchen so I could buy some of that delicious stuff! But I could buy Grand Manan dulse, and I did almost every day. Dulse is a purplish seaweed harvested at low tide on the rocks of Dark Harbor on Grand Manan Island off the south coast of New Brunswick, a few miles to the southeast of St. John. It is dried several hours and becomes a great treat, with a salty, tangy taste that is positively addictive. I would eat a 50-cent bag of it, about a medium-sized mixing bowl's worth, in several minutes. I thought that seaweed was the perfect food for a dieter -- virtually no calories -- until I inadvertently discovered a major drawback. I left some in my car on a warm day and found the odor it emitted positively chthonic!

The City Market housed Wilson's Fish Stall, Dean's Meat Stall, Fenwick Cheese and Poultry, Denton's Snack Bar, Lord's Fish Market, P.C. Raymond's Hams And Bacon, and B. London

Hampstead's, which sold vegetables and berries from rows of baskets. Other stalls sold strawberries, raspberries, and rhubarb.

I liked best Slocum And Ferris Fancy Groceries which combined a well-stocked, old-timey country store with a specialty, delicacy-food boutique. One could buy delicious candy, condiments for cooking, canned imported French truffles or escargots, Irish gooseberry jelly, tins of Scottish shortbread, and Norwegian "King Haakon" filled chocolate candies, among many other items. Fruits and vegetables were available in open bins outside the spacious, tidy expansive stall, fronted by a refrigerated case that displayed behind glass a wide variety of fish, red meat, and seafood, especially lobsters and scallops. The stout, jovial woman who tended the store sang Scottish folk songs as she made several sandwiches and wrapped them, mostly salmon sandwiches, at $1.60 each. She rang up purchases on an antiquated, embossed copper cash register that flanked the refrigerated display case.

Near the City Market, I often walked around King's Square, a park, the highest point of the downtown, where I enjoyed a changing view of the harbor. For example, looking down King Street I saw stevedores unloading large mobile-home-sized containers, as well as smaller containers -- "containerized cargo" -- onto the concrete wharf from red-and-white Canadian ships. On the opposite side of the square, looking down King Street North, I saw the harbor bridge in the distance, a graceful concrete-and-steel span supported by two huge concrete piers rising out of the water. Such views, that appear suddenly as one comes to intersections, are eye-appealing delights that St. John shares with San Francisco, another city compactly covering hills overlooking an important port.

From historical markers about the city, I learned that Benedict Arnold, whom I was taught in grade school was a traitor, lived and operated a business in St. John, where he was a hero, following the American Revolution of 1776. I also learned the first years in the fledgling settlement of St. John proved extremely hard for the Loyalists. Many died from the hardships. They had come en masse -- five thousand in a few ships -- as the cold weather was taking hold, fleeing Boston after the colonists who had wanted secession from Britain had won out and were determined to wreak vengeance on them, ranging from petty harassment to confiscation of property to tarring and feathering, to lynching. The 5,000 Loyalists, one third of Boston's population, disembarked within a few days onto the primitive St. John wharf.

It must have been an extremely bleak experience to look up at the towering, yellow-gray rock formations on which the few rude dwellings stood, the settlement still without streets, and realize that those forested crags had suddenly become their only home. I'm sure a good number of them had a good cry shortly after their arrival, asking themselves the question: How can I survive here? In fact, many did die during the first winter.

After two weeks in St. John that mixed pain with interesting experiences, I left 90 Mecklenburg Street for Grand Falls, Newfoundland. After the discomfort and desolation of a room in a ghetto that rivals the worst in Chicago, I was happy to leave. After room 1-A, with its roaches and filth, Grand Falls would prove a heaven.

My classes met in the local high school, Grand Falls Academy, which operated as the extension center in central Newfoundland for the Memorial University of Newfoundland, located in the capital, St. John's, on the East Coast. My roll call in Education 4360, Sociology of Education began with Catherine Balsom, R. Bruce Bowers, Harold Colin Budgell, Nina Butt, Sidney J. Coffin, Vera Coish, Mary Foley, and Elisabeth E. Foster. It ended with Bertha Prior, Joe Rideout, Brenda Roberts,

Allan Spencer, Edward "Ted" Trenchard, Kevin Verge, and Aloysius ("Just call me Al, pal.") Walsh.

The top of my Ed 4380, Philosophy of Education class list read: Doreen Andres, Elizabeth Ball, Judy Barlett, Shirely Boone, R. Bruce Bowers, Barbara Brake, and Nina Butt. The bottom was comprised of Donna Norman, Shirley Pinksen, Frank G. Ramjattan, and Emily Stoodley, the stylishly dressed, attractive, 54-year-old wife of summer session coordinator Roy Stoodley.

R. Bruce Bowers was a thin, alert, intellectual-looking young man who sat directly in front of me, in the first desk of the middle row, in both classes. When I think of my Newfoundland classes, I first conjure an image of Bowers – ramrod-erect posture, staid demeanor, laconic, dry class comments, and eyes constantly probing and darting at me from behind his thick glasses, like caplin glinting in the Newfoundland shoals in early June.

Frank G. Ramjattan, of East Indian descent, had come to Newfoundland from Trinidad. He had a rich, dark brown skin color -- the only person of color in the class. A good student, active in class discussion, he only missed class once. One morning he had fainted in Norris Arm, from where he commuted daily. Henry Rideout, one of his fellow commuters, had rushed Ramjattan to the hospital. Rideout later explained, "Frank didn't take his medicine for hypertension three days running."

M. Fred Parsons, a grade four Norris Arm teacher, commuted with Ramjattan and Rideout. He was built like a professional welterweight boxer, compactly slabbed with muscle that caused his tattoos to dance whenever he flexed his arms. After class one morning, Parsons stopped by my desk for a chat. "The only reason I'm commuting 70 miles round-trip for this damn course is money," he said. "If I pass, I get an increase on my $16,000 salary."

"Not very intellectual, eh?" I said.

"Intellectual, smintellectual! I have three kids and a wife to support. Do you?"

"No, only myself."

"Well," sneered Parsons, "you can see that Ed 4360 is more like $4,360 to my way of thinking. I don't give a whale's ass about Sociology or whatever this course is."

"I ought to fail you for disrespect of high, supreme, exalted professorial authority and American power. Have you no respect, man? Have you no fear?"

"Well b'y, you fail me and you get this t'ing here on your lips!" Parsons held a fist at me and flexed his right arm so a tattoo did a fancy, menacing two-step. "It's a fist kiss, this here, b'y!"

"What a lovely tattoo," I burbled, giving a nervous half-smile. "What an artistic thing, to have a work of art right on your body."

Sidney Coffin, a grade six teacher from Fogo Island, located near-in off the northeastern coast, enrolled in both my classes. He resided the entire summer in Grand Falls with his wife and two young daughters. He was a soft-spoken, unassuming, strait-laced family man who didn't mind expressing his opinions. He did not at all like the government's plan to construct a bridge from the Newfoundland coast to his island. "They ought to keep it the way it is," he opined. "Let the ferry carry people back and forth. That way we can keep our isolation. We can keep the riff-raff out. Once they get a bridge in, there'll be too many visitors and a lot of bad influences. I want my daughters to grow up the way I want them to. I don't want them on dope and becoming defiant. That would be a great tragedy for me."

"But wouldn't a bridge bring good things, too?" I asked. "Maybe you could still keep your lifestyle and benefit from a bridge, too?"

"It's a nice pipe dream, Dr. Heath, but it won't work. Once that bridge's in, they'll bring in a McDonald's Restaurant and then the gangsters, prostitutes, pollution and heroin will follow right behind. People'll eat so much junk food they won't know what good food is. Our kids will run in gangs and be on drugs and the fish will die off from the pollution. And pretty soon the government will have a toy or candy factory out there, or some darn thing. Thanks, but no thanks, Dr. Heath."

"But what'll you do if they do get it built?"

"I dunno. Cry a lot, I guess, and hope my daughters will be grown up enough by then so they can leave and find their own Fogo, so they can be as happy as we are out there now."

"I see, I see," I said. "Maybe they'll have to move north to Labrador, to get away from progress."

"That might help," returned Coffin, "but even up in Labrador they have a McDonald's now."

Mary Foley discovered two weeks into my philosophy class that she had diabetes and required treatment two mornings a week. I arranged for her to attend only three days a week and evaluated her on the basis of a longer term paper and a modified final exam. For the final, I seated her on the window side of the room and opened several windows for her and two pregnant students, who insisted they would faint if I didn't. Mary did very well in the course. I hope life has been good to her since the summer class and that she has mastered her malady.

The day before the final exam, one of the Norris Arm commuters, Helen Day (she didn't ride with Ramjattan, Rideout, and Parsons) phoned me, requesting permission to take the Philosophy of Education final at 9 a.m. rather than in the scheduled 1 p.m.slot. She explained that she had to leave Grand Falls early to catch the ferry to Fogo Island in order to attend an annual family reunion. Like the wonderful person and caring professor that I am, I made special arrangements for her to take an early test.

I told Sidney Coffin about Helen Day's Fogo reunion and noted, "If there'd been a bridge, she could've taken the 1 p.m. test like she was supposed to."

Sidney chuckled. "But that would be progress! People on Fogo don't care about four hours. We've been out there 400 years and four hours are of no concern to us."

An excerpt from the summer session schedule, featuring course and room assignments in Grand Falls Academy, follows:

Rm 301. English 405 A & B. Literature of Britain. Time, 9:00-11:00. Dr. Stan Freiberg.

Rm 303. Education 4360 – Sociology of Education. Time, 1-2 p.m. Dr. G. Louis Heath.
Education 4380 – Philosophy of Education. Time, 9-10 a.m. Dr. Heath.

Dr. Stan Freiberg, a white-haired, ruddy-cheeked professor of English, an American who taught at the University of Calgary, was a dynamic and popular teacher, a genial man of about fifty. A beautiful young lady in her late twenties, a former University of Calgary graduate student, had accompanied him to Newfoundland. They lived together in an apartment in Bishop's Falls, twelve miles east, and commuted daily in an ancient, drab Volkswagen bug that sounded like an unusually big bumblebee in a perpetual tailspin. The generation-gap-bridging couple got along famously and were fun to talk to at all the summer session social functions and around Grand Falls Academy.

Regarding intramural tension in the 45-member University of Calgary English faculty, Stan observed, "There is tremendous backbiting and infighting in my department. It can really get to you. That is why I get out of there in the summer and take these visiting assignments like this one in Newfoundland...We had Saskatchewan novelist W.O. Mitchell* in residence with us, and his son, Orm, too. Some of the people in my department were so

164

threatened by this creative pair that they did their best to run them off. They didn't give either enough time to write, which is what they thought they were coming for, to be writers-in-residence...W.O. was loaded up with creative writing students to supervise and a class to teach, and Orm was given two classes to teach. If I'd been chairman, I'd have simply let them write as much as they wanted as long as they kept office hours so that they would be a resource on campus...Orm was more acceptable to the department. He was more out of the scholarly mold than his father...My colleagues went out of their way to slight the Mitchells. They wouldn't even put W.O. Mitchell's novels on the department bibliography as being recognized Canadian literature, which they are...Finally, father and son got so disgusted they packed up and left...I guess they wonder why they were invited to Calgary in the first place. That's a good question."

(* From 1948 on, W. O. Mitchell lived in High River Alberta, 35 miles south of Calgary. He was born in Weyburn, Saskatchewan, where he lived to age twelve. The novel, **Who Has Seen The Wind**, published by Macmillan of Canada in 1947, that solidly established his reputation as an author, is set in small-town Saskatchewan.)

Following summer session, Dr. Freiberg was to begin the second sabbatical granted him by the University of Calgary. "I've been at Calgary ten years and this is my second sabbatical. Pretty good, eh?...My first sabbatical I went to Mexico and wrote poetry...I published my Mexican poems with Crest Press in Wisconsin."

Stan had also published a chapbook of his Newfoundland poetry with Crest Press. He lent me a copy, which both I and my landlady read. Mrs. Lind thought the poems not only good but accurate on details of the Island. For example: "He writes of the turquoise coves," she noted. "Turquoise is exactly the right word to describe the color of that water." The chapbook also featured several of Freiberg's color photos taken around the Island.

165

Before beginning his second sabbatical, he and his girlfriend were going camping along the Cabot Trail in Nova Scotia. She was to then travel to Toronto, to be with her family, while he went to Virginia to do research on a regional author. The next step was to meet in Chicago in December and drive to Houston to board a ship that would take them to a four-month sojourn in Chile and Peru.

On June 22nd, the Newfoundland Unemployed Teachers Association held its first meeting on the St. John's campus of Memorial* University. Inside a month, it claimed 625 members. The Depression in Teaching had come to the Island with a vengeance. The teaching credential was no longer a guarantee of a job. Newfoundland had begun to generate its own professionally educated proletariat.

(* "Memorial" refers to the dedication of the University at its founding to the memory of the many from Newfoundland who died in World War I, especially the 800 who died in a half-hour on July 1, 1916 at the Battle of Beaumont-Hamel in Belgium. Newfoundland has also memorialized those war dead by buying the farmland in Belgium where that battle was fought.)

I talked with summer session coordinator Roy Stoodley about this. "It looks like Newfoundland is beginning to produce its own class of educated people who can't find jobs," I remarked. "You're heading the way of India, which has a million educated people who are unemployed or underemployed."

Roy shrugged. "It's quite a development. It wasn't too long ago that I couldn't fill out my staff at Grand Falls Academy. Every year I was two or three teachers short. Now I get at least 75 applications for every job. I knew a long time before the Newfoundland Unemployed Teachers Association started that there were a lot of jobless teachers around."

"Where will they go? What will they do?" I asked.

"They'll have to find work outside teaching, here in Newfoundland or upalong. Most likely upalong as jobs are more scarce here than in the rest of Canada, eh."

I chuckled, then grimaced. "I see. Then their education is a lost cause?"

Roy nodded glumly. "It always was, sort of, economically anyway. I began teaching in Grand Falls in 1948 at a salary of $1,200 a year, which was considered a very good teaching salary." He gave a short, humorless laugh. "But the janitor at the school made $1,500. He made twenty-five percent more because the school had to offer him a competitive wage or else he'd leave to go work at the Abitibi paper mill."

"Even then a total loss," I muttered.

"Always the bottom, in good times or bad, we teachers," mused Roy in a poetic lilt. "Back in those days a lot of teachers worked summers in the mill so they could make $1,500, the same as the janitor, for the year. It got a little demeaning, eh, the way the janitor lorded it over us, the way he felt superior, pushing a broom and waxing floors. It was disgusting."

"Except now it's worse," I added. "Now the teacher can neither teach nor get on at the mill. They've become their own class of professional, unemployed people."

"That's the way it looks," Roy said sadly. "That's the way it looks."

Roy and I hit it off well, as if there were a special family bond between us. When I reflect on it, maybe it was some special magic. After all, we had shared an important experience in local history. When Roy first came to Grand Falls in 1948, he too had rented from Mrs. Harriet Lind, a cottage behind her home that no longer stands. (Her husband, Jim, the Grand Falls city manager, was then alive.) Maybe a little of Mrs. Lind's grace, high intelligence, and congeniality had rubbed off on both our dour souls.

167

G. Louis Heath, Ph.D.

I'd like to someday meet Mrs. Lind's only child, Laurie, a professor of education at MacQuarie University near Sydney, Australia. I went to the mailbox daily for Mrs. Lind to look for "Laurie's aerogramme," which came every few days. She always rewarded me by sharing the news from down-under. I could tell from those letters -- as much as you can tell from letters anyway -- that Laurie, wife to British-born computer salesman Tom, and mother of two young daughters, Melissa and Diana, aged six and nine, was indeed her mother's daughter, a highly caring and intelligent person.

One of the term papers submitted in the Sociology of Education class concerned Newfoundland's unemployed teachers. It was Clifford Heartsill's "The Unemployed Teacher In Newfoundland," 16 pages, two tables, one map.

He reported that in June, 1976 there were 729 teachers out of work in Newfoundland. By June, 1977, that figure had risen, according to Canada Manpower, to 1,005. Heartsill, himself an unemployed English and Speech teacher, age 24, opined, "I attended university for five years and all I can qualify for is to take more classes...It is very depressing to me that I cannot practice what I have been trained to do, that I must survive by doing what part-time work I can get...Right now, I am a quarter-time clerk at Cohen's Furniture. Now I ask, Is that what five years at Newfoundland Memorial should lead me to?...I feel wasted, depressed, and angry...Sometimes I feel like lashing out and killing my professors..."

Heartsill went on to ventilate his angry disgust over Newfoundland Minister of Education Wallace House's recent statement that he could not in good faith encourage young people to select teaching as a profession. Heartsill urged all out-of-work teachers to organize a revolution to bring down the government of Newfoundland and introduce a socialist state "so that I can get a better job, one befitting the years of sacrifice I made to hone

168

my mind into a fine, razor-sharp instrument that can cut through all the crap around this Island."

The final day of class, Edwina Power rose and presented me with four gifts. "On behalf of both your classes I am giving you some gifts," she smiled. "We appreciate the great devotion you have put into your classes. You have provided us with great educational experiences. We appreciate it!" The class burst into spontaneous applause that really moved me. I had not gotten this kind of royal, wonderful treatment at the end of a class before in Canada. It was with a force of will that I kept from crying. I was very moved, visibly so, by their appreciation and generosity.

I opened my four gifts after I got back to Mrs. Lind's. The first three contained, as Mrs. Powers had said, books. The class knew how I loved to read Canadian books. The first book was **That Far Greater Bay**, a selection of humorist Ray Guy's columns for the St. John's **Evening Telegram**. That paperback had won the 1977 Stephen Leacock Silver Medal for the best humor published in Canada. I especially appreciated that gift because I had been guffawing my way through Ray Guy's hilarious columns, interlarded with sharp political comments, throughout the summer. Ray Guy could well be Newfoundland's most valuable resource. Others agree with me, because at age 44, in 1984, seven years after I left the Island, Guy was elected to the Canadian News Hall of Fame.

The second book was Dillon Wallace's **The Lure Of The Labrador Wild**, about a tragic, three-man 1903 American expedition into the Labrador interior that had become thoroughly lost and could not get out before the onset of cold weather. Leonidas Hubbard, Jr. starved to death while his companions, including author Dillon Wallace, suffered greatly from frostbite and malnutrition. I enjoyed this book because it is a great story of how men fared under incredible adversity.

The third book was Ted Russell's **The Chronicles Of Uncle Mose** (Breakwater Books, Portugal Cove, Nfld., 1975). The book is a collection of 37 radio scripts selected from Ted Russell's 600 "Uncle Mose" broadcasts from the fictitious, northeastern-coast fishing settlement of Pigeon Inlet on the CBC Fisheries Broadcast from 1953 to 1962. Uncle Mose, the narrator, lived among eccentric, equally fictional neighbors -- Grandma and Grampa Walcott, Levi Bartle, Skipper Joe, Jethro Noddy, and Aunty Sophy -- about whom he spun his yarns.

Cliff Russell, my landlady Mrs. Lind's brother-in-law, and retiring chairman of the Newfoundland Fisheries Loan board and relative of author Ted Russell, took me fishing on the Twillick River after summer school. We didn't catch a salmon but we had the greatest fun chatting as we waded into the water, casting artificial flies, and swatting away real mosquitoes.

The fourth gift consisted of a miniature six-pack of Newfoundland "Screech," retailed as a souvenir of the 1977 Canada Games in St. John's. "Screech" is rum imported from the Caribbean and bottled in Newfoundland as the quasi-official alcoholic beverage of the Island. It's supposed to be so potent that it makes you scream like hell - that is, screech - from the sheer misery of the stuff burning its way down your gullet and assailing the lining of your stomach. However, I never had such problems with the six 1.2-ounce bottles, which I imbibed in small draughts of not more than a half-ounce each over two weeks.

The labels on the miniature bottles of **Screech** read "Jeux Canada Games '77, St. John's/Terre-Neuve, Newfoundland/August 7-19 aout 1977," signaling an unprecedented provincial assertiveness and sophistication in the realm of self-promotion and tourism. Mrs. Lind observed that, in her seventy years on the Island, she had never seen any such Newfoundland souvenir marketed before. Perhaps the legacy of the 1977 Canada Games will increase the drawing power that Newfoundland exerts on prospective tourists. There is certainly room for improvement for, that summer, only one percent of the tourists who went to Nova Scotia took the ferry over the Cabot Strait to Newfoundland.

A week after my classes had ended, I received at Mrs. Lind's a card from my student Robert Pickett. It was a Rust Craft Studio Card, made in Scarborough, Ontario, costing 50 cents, and mailed at the then first-class postage rate of twelve cents. It read: "Goodbye and Good Luck! You'll Be Missed By One...And All! (Especially Me!), Robert Pickett." That card went straight to my heart and I have kept it in a secure place lo these many years.

Summer Expenses

Gas. The price I paid per Canadian gallon of regular averaged 98.9 cents. I ponied up $4.93 for 5.1 gallons at Travelways Shell on Highway 401 at Bowmanville, Ontario; $4.90 for 5.8 gallons at Bud's Gas Bar, Cornwall, Ontario; $4.75 for 4.9 gallons at Martinet Plaza Shell, La Pocatiere, Québec (where, as I visited their restaurant for a thermos of coffee, some prankster sprinkled a handful of broken glass about my brake pedal. I felt a sliver of it, far up into my instep, about an hour later, when the fiery debilitating pain of it forced me to stop quickly.); $3.15 for three gallons at Harley Kilcollins' Shell, Wicklow, New Brunswick; $4.70 for 4.8 gallons at T.J. Davis Shell in Young's Cove, New Brunswick; $6.00 for 6.3 gallons at the Texaco in Four Falls, New Brunswick; $5.40 for 5.1 gallons at Murray Chisholm Esso in Whycocomagh, Nova Scotia; $6.20 for 5.3 gallons at E and J Restaurant, Glovertown, Newfoundland; and. $5.80 for five gallons at Harnett's Service Station, Lewisporte, Newfoundland.

The prices demonstrate that the further north I drove, as I penetrated up into the Maritimes, the more expensive my fuel became. From the 85 to 95 cents range in Ontario and Québec, by the time I fetched up on the Island via the ferry from Nova Scotia, I had to pay over a dollar. In Grand Falls, throughout the summer, I paid. $1.04 8/10 per gallon of Canadian regular -- the Canadian gallon is 20 percent larger than the U.S. gallon -- at downtown Marsh Motors.

Oddments. A Canadian first-class stamp cost 12 cents. A copy of a **Grand Falls Advertiser**, the local newspaper, was 20 cents. The sales tax throughout the Maritimes was eight cents on the dollar and the Newfoundland hotel room tax bit into the wallet at a whopping 10 percent.

Hotels and Motels. My rooms averaged $12.17 a night. Room 303 in the YMCA Central Branch at 433 Wellington Street in London, Ontario was $7.50 plus 7 percent tax (The clerk told me smugly, "London is the city where the wine companies test out their new wines to see what the **normal person** likes."); $8.00, and 56 cents tax, went for room 231 at the Royal Hotel in Cornwall, Ontario ("Romeo Lefébvre, Mgr., D. Villeneuve, Clerk"); Chambre No. 112B in the Hotel Ottawa, St. Hyacinthe, Québec, cost $9.00 plus the 8 percent room tax, erroneously calculated at 90 cents, when it should've been, of course, 72 cents ("Jean & Roger Lefébvre, Props."); $9.75 at the Belevedere Hotel, Truro, Nova Scotia (Gwen Nyke, Clerk); $12.96, including 8 percent tax, at the Hotel Sussex, Sussex, New Brunswick ("T.L. Madden, Proprietor"); $10.00, plus 80 cents tax, for room 200, Grand Central Hotel, Edmunston, New Brunswick ("Mrs. Anna Hébert, mgr."); and, $17.50 to stay at the comfortable, remodeled Hotel Corner Brook on Main Street, Corner Brook, Nfld. ("The management will not be responsible for lost or stolen property or rape," jested the clerk, in very poor taste.) The steep Newfoundland hotel tax there ran my bill to $19.25. (overheard in the corridor outside my room: "I'm glad I divorced that woman. I was ready to kill her.")

My rent in Grand Falls for two-and-one-half months at 49 Carmelite Road, at Mrs. Harriet Lind's – "Hattie's" – was $5 a day. Widow Lind lived in an elegant, spacious, two-story white-and-green frame home. She was the best landlady I ever had and one of the finest people I ever met.

On the way home from Newfoundland, I spent a week in late August at St. Francis Xavier University in Antigonish, in northern Nova Scotia, where I stayed in room 627 of Chisholm

House in MacKinnon Hall, a stately brown sandstone building. Summer school had ended and the campus of elm-lined walkways and stone and brick buildings was quiet. The campus church flanked MacKinnon Hall and a dozen Mounties, attending a law-enforcement seminar, roomed on either side of me. Thus surrounded by the RCs and the RCMP, I deemed it highly advisable that I not deviate one whit from my usually impeccable behavior.

How could I? The first person I met on campus was a priest in black ecclesiastical garb with a white plastic front-to-back collar. He was sitting comfortably in a lawn chair in front of the infirmary reading the financial pages of the **New York Times.** He told me that 33 of the 206 faculty are priests, that the Catholic Church is the focus of campus life. He also gave me a detailed statistical rundown on faculty salaries. "I teach economics and history," he said in a contented tone. "I made $31,800 this year." The lively glint in his eyes impressed me as being inspired not only by his relationship to God but also as registering his quite decent academic salary, far higher than mine at Illinois State University.

As we talked, well-dressed young people, mostly twentyish, walked by on their way to church. Before 11 a.m. arrived that Sunday, a good hundred people passed by us on an elm-naved walkway. I asked the priest why he wasn't going to church, and he replied elliptically that he didn't have to. He didn't elaborate.

The small pleasant downtown of Antigonish nuzzled the southern edge of campus. Colonel Sanders Kentucky Fried Chicken and a place called the Pizza House were garishly visible, but tidy, unobtrusive Wong's Restaurant on Main Street served the best meals. "Silent Movie" played at the Capitol Theatre.

As for snacks, I could patronize Sobey's, IGA, or one of the three convenience stores on Main Street: Webb's, Corner Market, or Jim's One, the closest to campus. All were open seven days a week till midnight.

173

G. Louis Heath, Ph.D.

Most my time in Antigonish was not spent in town or on campus, but on the nearby beaches on St. George's Bay, which connects with the Northumberland Strait and the Gulf of St. Lawrence. The glistening, pure-white sand that looks like granulated sugar, and the chill blue water, the bluest I've ever seen, off Cribbens and Mahoney beaches, were a sheer delight for me throughout that week of warm, cerulean days.

Chapter 7

Lakehead University, 1978

I decided to travel to northwestern Ontario, to remote Thunder Bay, the summer of 1978. I had tried for a job there, at Lakehead University, in 1974, and was rewarded only with a frustrating nibble. However, four summers later, and with no summer job available, I remained intrigued with the isolated university in a city I had never visited. So, I reserved a room on the campus for the summer in order to do sociological research and work on my action-packed novel of high suspense and bloodcurdling thrills set in Montreal, Toronto, Berkeley, and a few places in between.

This chapter recounts my stay on the Lakehead campus, offering anecdotes about people I met and excerpts from my diary. I begin with entries about my travel from Illinois to Canada:

May 30, Tuesday. Up at 6:30 a.m. Prepare to leave. Clear blue sky. Simply beautiful day...As I drove north on I-35 toward Mason City, Iowa and Minneapolis, I was passed by an **empty** black hearse with open white curtains. The hearse took up a position a few yards ahead of me, in my lane, the right. Then a shiny Stygian black VW beetle passed me and occupied the lane immediately to the left of the hearse. I had my lights on, as I always do when I travel long distances, to make my beige VW more noticeable. With my lights on, traveling behind the hearse and the other VW in mourning black, I felt either part of a funeral procession or an ominous situation. A rare black VW bug and black hearse passing me and traveling shoulder to shoulder, as though to seal me off. Be careful, I thought, crossing myself. I want to get through this summer to September 4th and age 34. I don't want it, the end, to happen violently, on the road or anywhere, this summer.

175

G. Louis Heath, Ph.D.

I finished a leg of 419 miles today before I took a room in the Super 8 Lodge, Clear Lake, Iowa (on I-35, nine miles west of Mason City)...

May 31, Wednesday... Got 34.047 miles per gallon, better than the 31.13 and 30.86 mpg on the two fill-ups yesterday. Cool temps in the 40s, a light rain, and a breeze that reduced surface temperature and friction against the asphalt, cumulatively produced greater fuel and engine efficiency...I look forward to 20% greater mileage on the 20% larger Canadian gallon!...

June 1, Thursday.... Arrive 3:15 p.m. at Lakehead University in Thunder Bay, Ontario. Assigned to Men's Residence Hall #117. Nice residence overlooking a small, man-made lake, on the opposite shore of which lies a modern brick complex of structures that includes the student union...Men and women are mixed in this hall for summer session. I see African male students, fixing dinner in the common kitchen, a coed strolling about in a bathrobe, and a white male Canadian student lounging in a TV room...

This campus is set amid a primeval forest of spruce and fir, and various deciduous trees. I've been here a half-hour and already feel very cozy and comfortable...

June 2, Friday... My room has a grand view of a stand of tall stately firs that silhouette against the sky dramatically...I'm on the first floor, twenty feet from an asphalt path....Tennis court near my room...

June 3, Saturday... On the radio I heard several songs by a country singer named McAuliff who had been struck down with a cerebral hemorrhage at age 33 and died. Not to be morbid really, but first that damn hearse and black VW, and now this. And to think, I'll be driving a good many miles in my own beige bug before I can turn 34!...

5:30 p.m. I walk one hour along Golf Links Road to Red River Road where I find my way to Robin's Donuts. Kid presses his nose against the donut shop glass and breathes at me. Leaves fog that takes five or six seconds to disappear...57 degrees outside...

176

8:40 pm. Dinner at Chong Garden Restaurant, downtown Thunder Bay. I took the Arthur Street bus...I talked with a middle-aged Ojibwa Indian at Chong Garden. I mentioned Louis Riel and Gabriel Dumont. He said he'd heard them speak at a recent powwow. Now I really believe in Indians' ability to communicate with their dead ancestors!...

June 4, Sunday...Took 30 minute walk downtown. Dinner at Chong Garden...7 p.m. Saw Jane Fonda and Jon Voight in "Coming Home," about Vietnam disabled vets. Jane's husband, an officer, comes home to commit suicide in the ocean surf...Work on novel goes well...Red Rose tea bags make a very good tea...

June 5, Monday...6:30 p.m. Three mile walk on Arthur Street toward Kenora, Ontario, and back. About 50 minutes each way. Chinese dinner at Lotus Restaurant on Arthur Street, which is next to A&P, separated only by the Canadian Pacific's Red Oak Inn....

Bought $30.25 of groceries at A&P. Return to dorm at 9:30 p.m.....Arthur Street walk took me near a magnificent butte, Mount McKay. Very massive and beautiful...

June 6, Tuesday...Quite a few Indians around campus and in town...Bought 2 ¼ pounds of California plums at $1.39 a pound...Wrote, noon to 2:30. An excellent session. The murder begins to take shape. Good writing. This novel has pizzazz!...Light snack at student union cafeteria. Walked down Oliver Street to downtown Thunder Bay. Bought Mazo de la Roche's **Delight** at Co-op Bookstore ($1.95). Then I enjoyed an iced tea at Eaton's department store second-floor cafeteria. Forty minute return walk to campus in warm humidity with rain threatening. Wore Bermuda shorts and tennis shoes. Very casual. The convenience and leisure of summer -- dining, shopping, and walking when I wish to -- as opposed to living by the constraints imposed by the past terrible winter, the worst ever in Illinois history! The snow kept piling up so that I couldn't get my car into the alley behind my place for over a month! Unable to park in the garage, I had to park Old Illinois out front on the street, where she was regularly rudely swacked by plows clearing aside accumulated snow to enable traffic to pass...

8:30 p.m. $5.00 dinner at Lotus Restaurant, Arthur Street...

Down the hall from my room, lived Roger, a wheel-chair-bound victim of polio in his thirties. It was impossible for anyone along that hall not to get to know Roger, because he spent a great deal of time in the hallway bathroom, treating his greatly swollen limbs and taking care of his ablutions. Though he was in great pain that summer, and had to be in the hospital two weeks of it, the hundred-pounds-overweight, short, roundish man proved an excellent conversationalist. An outgoing person, he had a good many friends, including a girlfriend who helped care for him, taking him to the hospital and visiting daily.

"I'm having a big circulation problem in my legs," Roger said shortly after I arrived on campus. "It's very painful." I could see how they had to be. They looked twice as big as they should be and they were beet-red. His slacks off in the hallway bathroom, Roger was laving and toweling his legs, and plying them with packs of "blue ice." "This gives me a little relief," he said, "but it's only treating the symptoms. The cause is that I must sit all the time and I don't get the exercise I need."

"Have you tried isometrics, lifting yourself with your arms, or pressing against walls?"

"I've done some, but I keep backsliding, losing motivation. I can't seem to keep it up."

"What about a diet?"

"My doctor wants that, too. I've been losing a little. But it's difficult."

Roger had been a student at Lakehead nine years, majoring in accounting. His regular hospital visits, and, I think, an inclination to make the student life his career, had extended his undergraduate studies from 1969 to 1978, from his 24th birthday to his 33rd year, and he was but a junior. Since Lakehead

University was established in 1965, Roger's student career coincided with most the history of the University.

Often I saw Roger driving his motorized wheelchair along the sidewalks and streets in Thunder Bay. As he whirred by, I thought of how he might be struck by a car. When I mentioned my fear for him, he said, "Gary, I've been through many operations. I am full of pins and covered with scars, and I have had doctors make major mistakes on me in surgery, making my digestion of meals painful. So, I don't view it as a danger. It's one of the things I must do to be mobile in the vicinity of campus. I've fallen out of my chair onto the ice on the worst winter days and cars have just missed me, but that's the risk I'm willing to take. I like life, but if a car wiped me out, it wouldn't be such a bad way to go. It would end the pain."

One of Roger's favorite pastimes was to watch the daily rerun of a "M.A.S.H." episode on TV. He loved that series. "I've never seen a bad episode of M.A.S.H.," he smiled. "Alan Alda as Hawkeye really makes the series click. He's a great actor."

Occasionally, I ran an errand for Roger, especially to fetch a container of cube ice from the ice machine at the front desk so that he could pack his legs in it. (He had a pack of "blue ice" but had to rely on the front desk to freeze it for him. In the intervals, he used cube ice.) Every time I saw him cool down his distended limbs, I inwardly winced. Polio is a cruel disease, and Roger had forced me to be more empathetic to those who must bear that terribly heavy cross through their lives, often shortened by the duress imposed by their cross.

After knowing Roger, I'm especially gung-ho for spending public money for any and all facilities on campuses and elsewhere to make it possible for the disabled to get higher education and lead more productive lives, holding down good jobs and raising families.

"I love children," said Roger glowingly. "I want to have at least two of my own once I've finished my degree and have gotten myself established in accounting, and, of course, have married."

June 18, Sunday…10 a.m. Breakfast at Landmark Inn in the County Fair Shopping Mall. Young Québec couple, dressed for the outdoors, their backpacks on the floor at their table, had breakfast nearby. Hour walk in residential area surrounding mall…

1-4 p.m. Write eleven pages on my novel. Good pace. Exciting stuff. I like the suspense I've developed.

4:10 p.m. Walk downtown. Dinner at Chong Garden.

4:20 p.m. Saw Kirk Douglas in "The Chosen." Some frumpy asshole woman in the row behind me tells me not to chew my gum so loud. I give her the finger, and she viciously slaps my hand. My digit stinging, I quickly extend another finger at her, then move to another row posthaste.

Ran into Farzam, Iranian pre-med student, downtown after movie. We had coffee in Appollonaire Restaurant and talked an hour, taking the bus home together. A warm, lively, sensitive young man. He's off to Winnipeg soon for a course there…

June 23, Friday…Up at 10 a.m. Electricity off in Lakehead U dorms today. Beautiful bright sky slants through window, so plenty of light to read by. Read from Hugh Garner's **Cabbagetown**…

Lunch. Long talk with Farzam, Iranian science student, 21, who insists I look at least 40. He's a little too forceful and insulting about it, and I tell him that with his full black beard he looks a least 50.

Walk to Westfort Hotel Restaurant via South Edward Street. A tall line of grain elevators dominates the skyline in West Fort William, bearing the legend "Ft. William Elevator Co." They comprise a rank of sentries, of a concrete sort, at the end of Edward Street…

June 24, Saturday. Up at 8 a.m. Overcast. Ten died in plane crash near St. John's, Newfoundland yesterday. Seven were historians en route to St. Anthony's on the northwest peninsula to install a plaque commemorating an ancient Viking settlement, perhaps the first in North America. Plane ripped through the trees at the edge of a canyon and disintegrated into many pieces...

11 p.m. Late night meal of egg foo yong at Chong Garden, downtown Port Arthur ward of Thunder Bay. Talked half-hour with miners (nickel and iron) from Wawa, Ontario, 300 miles east, also situated on Lake Superior. $8.20 an hour wages. They're out on the town, having a good time. One said he's been divorced three times. At 37, he's already graying, and he claims he's finished with women...

At lunch one day in University Centre, I talked with Émile, a Lakehead University associate professor of business who was, he said, "very research-oriented." He told me, "I've been doing a lot of research on student fast-food patterns."

"Fast-food patterns? What are those?"

Émile smirked, as though I were stupid. "Fast-food patterns are the loci of the behaviors students embark upon in the matter of which pre-prepared provender they ingest."

"The junk food they eat?"

Émile furrowed his brow thoughtfully, and after several seconds said, "Yes, the junk food they eat. I never thought about putting it that way."

"Tell me more about your research. It intrigues me."

"It's questionnaire research at the pizza restaurants and the hamburger bars. Students are asked to fill out inventories about their background and why they chose pizza or hamburgers."

"Waddya find out?"

"A distinct dichotomy between lower class people, the freshmen and sophomores, and the upper class, juniors and seniors. The lower class prefer pizza because it sticks to their ribs better, because it seems to fill them up better. They are really into the cheese and anchovies!

"And the upper classpersons, they like hamburgers because they are even faster than pizza. They say hamburgers save them those important extra few minutes they need each week to get everything done. They are especially interested in a slice of pickle and tomato on their burger. They have more sophisticated tastes than the lower class."

"Hmmmm, pickle and tomato," I drawled. "Sounds ritzy." I paused, nonplussed. "But what is the value of such a finding?"

"Because of my research, the companies can target their advertising. The pizza companies can shoot for the freshman and sophomores and the hamburger chains can aim for the juniors and seniors."

"How can they do that? Sounds difficult to me."

"Well, for example, I've found also that juniors and seniors more often drive cars. So, that means the hamburger chains would do well to erect roadside signs to cry their wares, eh. But this would not be a good move for the pizza people. They'd be better off to buy advertising on the insides and outsides of our city busses for their target clientele. Students who don't own cars tend to take busses more often, statistically speaking."

"You otta publish these findings," I gushed. "You should share them with other business professors."

"I do. I put out a newsletter that I call the **Fast Food Market Research Report.** Over a hundred companies and 25 professors subscribe to it."

"You're a big name then?"

"I'm one of the tops in my area of expertise," Émile responded proudly. "And I'm on my way up. I applied to become Dean of the Business Faculty at Western Ontario University. I've built up my vita so well here that I feel I have a good shot at the job."

"You're building success on pizza and hamburgers," I noted. "A fast-food expert moving up fast!"

Émile nibbled on his tortilla that was the featured item on the cafeteria menu. "I hope," he said quietly.

"What's your opinion of these tortillas?" I asked, observing his lack of gusto in eating his.

"For students only," Émile returned laconically. "You might throw them to the lower class, but never to the seniors. Let them eat hamburgers."

"JUNK FOOD"

(a two-line short story by Professor G. Louis Heath)

"Dinner is served," said the tortilla to the pizza.
"Shall we have student?" asked the pizza of the hamburger.

June 27, Tuesday...12:30-1:45 p.m. Talked with the talkative Iranian pre-med student, Farzam. He says 85% of all Canadians under 25 have or have had V.D., a statistic I wouldn't believe if he paid me. He's fun and easy to talk to though. All this over lunch...

9 p.m. Canadian radio program on Woody Guthrie and Cole Porter. Long, detailed, excellent. I didn't know Porter was from Peru, Indiana, etc. It's nice to know. But I do wish I could learn more about Canadian culture on Canadian radio...After programs on Porter and Guthrie, I listen to one on "Bauhaus," the post WWI school of architecture and design founded by Walter Gropius in 1919...

June 29, Thursday...Dorothy Livesay, poet born in Winnipeg, 1909. Don Harron interviewed her on radio about her autobiography, **Right Hand, Left Hand.** She read some of her impressive poetry which expressed great antipathy toward fascism and immense concern for workers. She now has a grant to write about growing up in Toronto in the 1920s...

At lunch, I met Allen, a French prof here, and Abdul, a prof of classics. Allen's doing research on the French language as used in NW Ontario. Abdul, who looks Ojibwa but is an Arab, is teaching summer school. Excellent conversation. They pointed out the Lakehead U president's kid who graduated top in his class from this university at age 16. He took his degree in physics and is now a young teenaged graduate student, a phenom. He always sits alone, eats quickly, and talks with no one. A great prodigy. At 16, I was struggling through my junior year in high school...

June 30, Friday...4-6:30 p.m. Excellent writing session. Nine good pages on novel. Very exciting, compelling stuff!...Celebrated with a purchase of six brownie fudge squares, two mocha tarts, and three "hermit" cookies. Ate one tart, plus drank one quart skim milk at South Edward Street Cow Palace. Plus one ice cream bar, which I also bought there.

Then to the County Fair Plaza where I bought Robertson Davies's **Fifth Business** ($1.95). He wrote a book on Stephen Leacock, and also a preface to a book of selected stories by Leacock. I was earlier impressed with his writing, and my initial observation has been borne out by reading the first three chapters of **Fifth Business.** I read them in a coffee shop where I drank and consumed a 35-cent, single-scoop maple walnut ice cream cone, all this while my car sat in the mall parking lot with the headlights left inadvertently on!...

Home at 9 p.m.

The big floor fan I bought a couple days ago for $16.88 – two speeds — at Zeller's is proving very effective for my room. I have no complaints about the weather and my physical comfort so far...

July 12, Wednesday...Read Mazo de la Roche's **Jalna At Morning** till 11:30 a.m. To lunch at University Centre where I have the $1.50 special of sphagetti and meat sauce. Talked with Farzam a half-hour. He explained to me the outbreak of human venereal disease -- so he claims! -- among cows, horses, collies and other dogs, as we dined. His comments on VD are in extremely poor taste at mealtime, and I don't believe a word...

Two pages on novel finished at 7 p.m., at which time I walk to Kangas Saunas & Coffee Shop. Dinner at Kangas...Returned at 9 p.m. Attended Michael's (another Iranian) basement party. Danced, talked, and drank beer till midnight. Danced with a local non-college woman employed at Zeller's, and with Liz, a forestry major who's a residence assistant and lives next door to me...

July 13, Thursday...9 p.m. At Kangas, a young fellow 75 pounds overweight sits across the horseshoe-shaped counter from me. By watching him eat, I can tell how he got fat. First, a chocolate milkshake slurped down wolfishly. Then a quick, oleaginous hamburger, followed by a cigarette. He next orders a mammoth piece of chocolate cake. After this, another cigarette. The guy is maybe 25, and seems on his way to eating and smoking his way into a middle-age grave. He's having another cigarette as I write this into the 3 ½ inch by 6 inch F. W. Woolworth 50-sheet memo book that I carry around in my back pocket for diary entries.

July 17, Monday... After eating a $3.75 beef stew meal at Eaton's, I went at 1:20 p.m. to Cumberland Book Store at 12 Cumberland Street and bought Hugh Garner's **Murder Has Your Number** ($9.95) and Thomas H. Raddall's **His Majesty's Yankees** (paper, $3.50). I also bought **Historic Lakehead**, a pamphlet for $1.50.

I walked the two or so miles from downtown back up the hill to my car at Robin's Donuts...

2:30 p.m. -- To Canadian Imperial Bank of Commerce to withdraw $150. Then to the University Book Store where I purchased Stephen Leacock's **Frenzied Fiction** and Farley Mowat's **Never Cry Wolf**...

July 18, Tuesday...1 p.m. I got a haircut, downtown Thunder Bay, for $5. I enjoyed talking in the barber shop with a retired Abitibi paper mill accountant, a good conversa-

185

tionalist...Walked to Robin's Donuts, picked up car, drove to County Fair Plaza. Got $15 of dimes at the Bank of Montreal in order to xerox four chapters of my novel...

8:30 p.m. Arrive at Kangas on foot. Hot and humid inside café. Eat a beef sandwich, drink a diet cola. Such a nice restaurant interior. It's done in a Finnish modern style, very rugged and functional with much blonde pine surface and lots of carpet. Run by Finns.

On the way back, I feel in a buoyant mood, and I bare my teeth at a malamute tethered to a porch by a long leash. I growl and lower my head in mock attack. And the dog returns the attack, for the leash is not tied to anything. I had to run and dodge into and out of city traffic for about 100 yards before he finally gave up the chase, when, fortunately, his leash got hung up on a municipal bus sign. He got no blood out of me, though he did rip a lower pant leg. Thank God he wasn't a **real** attack dog, the kind trained to rip your throat out...

July 19, Wednesday. Up at 9:30 a.m. after 28 degree Celsius high yesterday (terribly hot), with high humidity that made my room uncomfortable...

5:30 p.m. - Dinner at University Centre. Talked with Greg Albert, who lives in the Men's Residence, room 155. He's a principal in Rainy River, Ontario, a hamlet of 1,300. He told me he's taking Native Studies courses in order to innovate, something he has to do in order to survive in his position. He's been principal 1 ½ years, and takes courses at Lakehead to eventually advance, if only to another principalship, after his time is up where he's at. He makes $26,000 per annum...

9 p.m. Walk half-hour down to Kangas Saunas and Coffee Shop on Oliver Street. On TV, watch Hamilton Tiger Cats come from a 23-3 deficit to defeat Saskatchewan Rough Riders 27-23. Ate two salmon open-face sandwiches at a dollar each and two coffees (35 cents; refill for 25 cents). Watched 11 p.m. news out of Duluth on cable, first time I've seen it in Thunder

Bay…Walking down and returning up Oliver Road, there was a brisk wind coming in off Lake Superior…

The most notable person I met in the laundry room that summer was Marvin, a barrel-chested redhead with a bristly beard, originally from the Yukon, who had been a member of Canada's ill-starred, ill-advised, peacekeeping mission in Vietnam. Marvin didn't talk about Vietnam, but he was voluble about his personal problems which stemmed, he said, from his fighting in Indo-China.

"My doctor says I have post-traumatic stress syndrome. I can't seem to concentrate and people frighten me. I never relax…My doctor says it's good for me to talk to people like you. He says it's good for me to get my anger out and not bottle it up. That's why I come here to do my wash. I meet people, mostly young people."

Marvin spoke with great visceral intensity and he gave off an aura of high compulsiveness, an electric sense that he was just barely holding on to a small center of himself and was about to fly off in an unpredictable direction. He was scary because he gesticulated by brandishing before his chest and face a hunting knife he had pulled from a sheath strapped to his ankle underneath his jeans. He had been using it to cut chunks from a huge wedge of watermelon when I arrived. With the knife, he gesticulated with great animation, to emphasize the forceful outpouring of his words. Eerily, he seemed to think not of the knife as a weapon. It seemed to be only a part of his gestures, and he was not, consciously anyway, trying to menace or harm me. However, I did not recognize this for quite some time, and I was braced tensely to do whatever I could to disarm him and defend myself whenever he attacked.

I had once thought that his order of problems were only those of the American Vietnam vets. Yet, there he was before me, a Canadian vet, tending his load of wash and talking like an ancient steam locomotive clanking feverishly and falteringly along. He punctuated his words with knife gestures as he ate chunks of watermelon and, as I sat on the edge of my chair with a rapidly beating heart and a galvanized skin the electricity from which could've illuminated a ball park for a night game. Finally, I concluded that the poor man was just eating watermelon!

"You're not a student?" I asked.

"Hell no. I didn't even make it through high school. I come up here to do my wash and talk, like I just told you."

"You don't seem to have problems to me," I lied, wishing to avoid saying anything that might set him off.

"Oh, but I do have problems, eh. My doctor prescribes some very powerful drugs for my problems. If I don't take what he gives me, I lose control."

"Lose control?"

"Bar fights, things like that. I'm spozed to stay out of bars, or else they'll take me off probation. I hurt a guy in a fair fight downtown and they gave me probation. I know they're watching me pretty close."

Marvin told me something of his Yukon past. "I grew up trapping and hunting. I made my living as a guide for hunting parties before I joined the army. It's still how my father makes a living...I'd never go back to the Yukon and be with my father again. I hate him more than ever after Vietnam. I thought I'd get over my hate for him in the army, but it only got worse...If I could ever get my head clear, so I could move ahead in my life, that'd be good. But right now, I'm very screwed up and fighting to keep myself together...I live downtown in an old hotel. It's the only thing I can afford, living down there with the other people on the garbage pile of life.

"It seems no one gives a damn for me. I got nothing to look forward to. That's what bothers me most, more than the drugs and my ulcers and the operations I've had on my brain and stomach. If I only could get my head together enough so I could hold down a job and get married, maybe that'd be enough for me. I don't wanna die a bum, like I am now, eh, down in that old hotel with all the mice and cockroaches running around."

On gorgeous, balmy, azure Dominion Day, Sunday, July 1, I took the Thunder Bay municipal bus downtown, sitting in the front, near the driver. Soon the driver and I were engaged in conversation. "I get paid extra today," smiled the young man of 35 or so.

"How much?"

"Double time and a half."

"Double time and a half!"

"Yes, eh. Double time because it's a holiday and a half more because it's Sunday."

"That's darn good for a little Sunday driving and hardly anyone taking the bus." Only one other person rode the bus from campus down the hill the couple miles to downtown and only three or four got on and off for shorter trips as we moved. "How much does your pay come to for today?"

"$220."

"Damn, that's good. I make only $75 a day. I'm a teacher, a college teacher."

"I used to be a teacher," the driver told me. "All the crap from the bureaucracy and the students, the low pay, the discipline problems, the drugs, they all took their toll. I quit after two years."

"And became a bus driver," I continued for him.

"No, not right away. First, I went to work for one of those federal anti-poverty programs, where you're spozed to do whatever you're spozed to do. I never could figure out just what I was spozed to do and neither could they. So, I quit there, too. At least I know what I'm spozed to do here: Drive from point A to point B, and back from B to A. And make twice the money!"

"You mean you were working in an agency that was trying to eradicate poverty and they were lost about what to do?"

"Absolutely. We had federal money and our mandate, eh, but no real objectives. We had to figure out how to eradicate poverty. Well, just try that one, eh. It's like trying to answer the question, 'Why is there air?' So, all we did was fret our time away in meetings discussing how to help poor people. We didn't come up with anything new…We concluded that Canadian society is class-stratified and that the poor people are at the bottom." The driver shrugged. "But we did fight one kind of poverty very successfully, our own, by pulling down decent salaries as we babbled."

"You should've had me on staff," I said. "I know how to abolish poverty. All you have to do is hire poor people in federal projects as consultants on poverty. Then they'll have incomes."

The driver chuckled. "Ouch, that hurts. It hits home a little too close. I really needed that anti-poverty job when I got it. Without it, I wouldn't have been able to pay my bills."

"Y'see, it works!" I enthused. "**Your** program worked!"

"For some anyway. For me anyway," opined the driver. "Us middle-class types temporarily out of a job. But for the hard-core poor, you can forget it. Some of them are illiterate, schooled only through grade seven or eight, if that. They have no education, no future. Some have poor health. They have nothing to offer. They have to go on welfare. They fall through the proverbial cracks in the economy and the dole keeps them eating."

We soon gave up discussing poverty and I asked, "Don't you get a little bored driving this thing? It's such a defined route you have. It's not like you're exploring."

"I don't get bored. Not yet anyway, after three years. I get to talk with lots of people like you, eh."

July 21, Friday…At 6:30 p.m., I listened to "As It Happens." They make phone calls to people involved in the news, especially "the States," as the program refers to the USA. They ask pointed, hard-hitting questions; e.g. they called a reporter on Long Island who is a specialist in spy reporting. He says that there are talks going on in Vienna to exchange a convicted Soviet dissident for two minor Soviets imprisoned in the U.S., despite Soviet denials…

Talked with Fong tonight, an engineering student from Hong Kong, whom I met on a city bus the second day after he arrived in Canada. He was wondering at the time how he'd survive here.

When he landed at Thunder Bay Airport, he could only see trees and wondered what he was getting into. ("This is a very small town, too small for me. It's a shock, flying from Hong Kong to here. Like landing on the moon, it's so different.") His father sends him money to study, and he estimates he'll need $5,000 for the first year here. ("It's **very** important for me to study, to study **very** hard. I don't want to miss my chance here. Lots of my friends are now working in factories.") Fong's father works in a bank...

July 22, Saturday... Young Chinese woman student in the hall is feeding several dollars of dimes into pay phone to call Washington, D.C...

5-6:30 p.m. Dinner in University Centre cafeteria. Dine and talk with the engineering bunch, all older fellows in their late twenties and thirties who are enrolled in an accelerated bachelor's degree program. One of them talked about his military service experiences. He told of a "donkey show" he saw in Germany that featured a donkey on roller skates fornicating with a young German woman also on roller skates. My stomach queased about and I vowed never to eat with the engineering clique again. Fabricated story or not, they're even worse than Farzam!

Another engineer recounted his Canadian Navy experiences as his contribution to the table talk. There was a fire at sea four years ago and one sailor died. A funeral service was held, and the man's earthly remains were slid into the sea. However, the person who had prepared the coffin had forgotten to drill holes in it and he had forgotten as well to put in the lead weight that would take it to Davey Jones' Locker. "We added the holes and lead the coffin needed as it floated away by firing about 500 rounds of machinegun ammo into it...Our enfilade made the funeral work and we had a great time!...."

I walked down the hill with "Rick," a young sailor (recent biology graduate of McMaster University in Hamilton, Ontario). He earns $1,300 a month. His ship has been carrying sodium sulfate ("acid soda") to bleach wood pulp at local paper mills.

191

Rick had just seen the film, "The Network," on campus, and as I was walking by as the movie crowd exited, he fell into step with me on Oliver Road, and tried to strike up a conversation "about the movie we just saw." I told Rick he had inferred incorrectly; I had not seen the movie. But I was on my way (9 p.m.) to Kangas for a snack.

Rick told me he was returning to the seedy part of downtown where he stayed in an old hotel where other sailors roomed. He was clearly very lonely, marking his time in port waiting for his ship to unload, load, and depart for Duluth. I bought him a cup of tea and we talked a few minutes at Kangas. I got the feeling he would've liked to talk hours....

July 23, Sunday...4 p.m. -- Chinese dinner at Lotus Restaurant on Arthur. "Dinner for one, $5."

5 p.m. -- Kicked soccer ball about on front lawn with Farzam and security guard...

7 p.m. -- Walk to town for exercise and the view. Take bus back. Ojibwa Indian boards bus, pays fare, takes a seat. A few seconds later he jumps up like an electric current has just entered his body. He runs down the aisle, forces his way out the side doors, and sprints down the middle of Arthur Street, cutting into an alley. Now what was that all about?....I can't engage the Ojibwa on campus in conversation. They sequester themselves in the University Centre cafeteria and elsewhere about campus, very aloof and wary. I can understand that, I think, at least a little bit. They have good historic and contemporary reasons for their aloofness, if that is anywhere near the right word. However, the Ojibwa on the bus posed an especially stunning mystery. I have no idea of what was running through his mind...

July 24, Monday... Worst riot in a hundred years at Pontiac prison in Illinois. Three guards killed. A terrible crime, the slaughter of those guards, and my heart goes out to their families!...

4 p.m. -- I go to the Canadian painters' exhibition at the National Exhibition Centre, off Gold Links Road, on the campus of Confederation College. Emily Carr's "Kitwancool Totems" is

a part of the show. Also included is a painting by each member of "The Group of Seven": Frank Carmichael, A.J. Casson, Lawren Harris, A.Y. Jackson, Edwin Holgate, Arthur Lismer, J.E.H. MacDonald, F.H. Varley, and Tom Thompson. Thompson (1877-1917) drowned at age 40 at the height of his artistic power. He was maybe the most brilliant of the group. There actually were more than seven (9), as new members replaced the deceased, and it just so happened the group always numbered seven. They all share with Emily Carr a compelling vibrancy in their paintings that interpret the Canadian landscape in such a way that I instinctively gravitate to them, trying to get intimately close, rather than passively viewing. These oils have "soul!"

July 25, Tuesday...5:30 p.m. -- Over dinner in University Centre, I talked with several women teachers, mostly from Dryden, Ontario, one of whom lives on my hall but is moving because of the loud music. She's taking Native Studies courses...I talked at length with another woman, a teacher from Atikokan, Ontario, who had adopted two children. One had committed suicide. She and her husband had gotten him when he was five years old, although the government said it was sending a two-year-old. The other child was also a government foul-up. The agency had said a blond, blue-eyed baby was coming. They went down to meet the train on which their bundle of joy was arriving on a January day of 50 below zero. When they looked beneath the folds of the baby blanket, they found a dark-haired, dark-eyed baby. "It's the government. They're always making mistakes like that," the Atikokan woman said philosophically...

Petits fours went with dinner tonight. They were left over from the reception for the new Lakehead University president...

July 26, Wednesday...Nigeria withdraws from the Commonwealth Games that begin in a week in Edmonton...

July 27, Thursday...Canada loans $1 billion dollars to Panama to develop their copper industry. They must buy Canadian equipment...

Noon -- I talked with three local firefighters at lunch, who make $19,000 a year. They work four days of ten hour shifts,

G. Louis Heath, Ph.D.

then four days off. They were on campus to play tennis on University courts...

July 28, Friday... Throughout the summer, the U.S. dollar is worth 10% more than the Canadian dollar. But, if a Canadian visits the States, the motels and restaurants discount his dollars 15%. Overheard tonight at the Voyageur Restaurant on West Arthur Street: "The bastards! They complain about us, but look what they did to me. They devalued my money by 15%!..."

July 29, Saturday... The several Iranians who reside in this hall spend a lot of time tinkering with, repairing, an old, bright-red, dilapidated car that is parked always in front of the residence...

July 30, Sunday...11 a.m. Listened to interview of Québec writer Roche Carrier. He says Québec has gone back to worshipping Maurice Duplessis, the heavyhanded premier of the province during the 1930s. This portends, he thinks, "a turning back in," a new isolationism....Carrier reads his best unpublished story, "The Hockey Sweater." Carrier's three books available in English translation are: **Fleur-de-lys, Where Are You?; Garden Of Delights;** and, **No Country Without Grandfathers.**

July 31, Monday... Cumberland Street downtown, three blocks on either side of Chong Garden Restaurant, is Thunder Bay's skid row. It teems with Indian, mostly Ojibwa, drunks, bums, and panhandlers. ("D'you have a quarter to spare?" is their most frequent approach.) They congregate particularly in the vicinity of Chong Garden. I saw one Indian so dead-drunk on the sidewalk, so lifeless, that I actually thought he may've been dead until I felt for and found a pulse. I called an emergency medical service number and told them they had someone who might die if he weren't put into a detoxification program. The woman who took my call said, "We can't respond to every Indian drunk in Thunder Bay as a medical emergency! We would have no time left over for real emergencies!..." She must have thought I was an Indian!

August 1, Tuesday....4 p.m. -- Play tennis with three students, doubles, on the court in front of the residence hall. We played several games over an hour and a half under the warm, humid, clear sky...

Cincinnati Reds' third baseman Pete Rose hits in his 49th consecutive game, tying the 1897 record held by Willie Keller (all-time pro record is held by American League's Joe DiMaggio, 1941).

11 p.m. -- I watch the news on the residence hall TV, the CBC's "The National," Peter Kent, anchor.

12 midnight. -- I watch the CTV's version of the news with anchors Harvey Kirck and Lloyd Robertson...CTV has by far the better newscast, I think...

August 3, Thursday...11 a.m. On local radio, CBQ, AM 80 on the dial, listen to Jim Wright with "Morningside in the Summer." Program on the Great Depression consisting of little-known facts such as: Miniature golf courses began in the Depression. Backgammon was big. Men worked in the Ontario forestry camps for 20 cents a day. And jokes such as:

During the Depression, two fellows, who had a joint bank account, hold hands and jump out of a hotel window to their deaths...Very dark humor, indeed!

3:45 p.m. I took a two-hour harbor cruise on the **Welcomeship** for $4. I met a couple with a young daughter from eastern Ontario (both French-speaking. She's a RN; he's a teacher, including the teaching of English as a second language). I enjoyed part of the trip in their company. Beautiful, sunny day but strong winds off the lake, so I stayed below deck, inside. Only a handful on this cruise compared to the number disembarking from the previous trip. To the northeast we went as far as the Abitibi paper mill. To the west, we went into the short McKellar and Mission Rivers, and then up the Kaministikwia River...Sixteen huge grain elevators serve the harbor.

A Yugoslav and a Soviet ship were docked before the elevators. Our tour guide said the Soviets were loading malt.

On the way to the **Welcomeship** cruise, I walked down the hill, falling in step with a Canadian Ph.D. in Economics, Mark. (B.S., Lakehead; Ph.D., Queen's University in Kingston, Ontario). Mark recently finished working his first year for Bell Telephone in Montreal and makes $25,000. He started at $21,600. His hometown is Thunder Bay. He's home on a visit to his mother and father, a railroad worker. The family is Ukrainian...

August 5, Saturday...Worst bus disaster in Canadian history. Over 40 die as the brakes fail and bus hurtles into a lake...From the second floor of the University Centre, I can see eight grain elevators in a compact row on the Port Arthur ward waterfront...Thunder Bay is divided into Port Arthur ward and Fort William ward...

August 6, Sunday...Anniversary of that day of infinite terror when the equation E=mc squared began to hang over the human race like the sword of Damocles. Hiroshima!...

Lunch, 11:30 a.m. to 1 p. m. - Talked over lunch with Jeff Retcio, business teacher from Sault Ste. Marie, Ontario. He's 39 and makes $30,000 after 14 years on the pay scale. This includes $2,500 for serving as chairman of a department of six. He's had the niece of famous Harvard Professor and author John Kenneth Galbraith in one of his classes. (Galbraith and I share an important past: both of us stayed at International House during our Ph.D. graduate school years at the University of California at Berkeley. He in the 1930s; I in the 1960s. For all I know, we may have even lived in the same room. During my three-and-a-half years at "I House" -- pronounced "Eye House" -- I lived in three different rooms. So, minimally, I lived in very close proximity to where the very famous Ontarian Dr. Galbraith once resided.)

Jeff noted that many teachers in "The Soo" take Easter break vacations in Cuba, the Caribbean, Hawaii, etc., for the status they believe such vacations confer. "I and my wife don't go in for those trips...A shopping trip in Michigan suffices for her."

Jeff is taking an M.Ed. degree at Lakehead, for "the job security potential, as well as the educational value...So that a young guy can't come in and be too much of a threat to me as department chairman."

1:30 p.m. – Drove east on the Trans-Canada to Pass Lake turn-off. Turned right, and drove out on Sibley Peninsula ("Sleeping Giant" mountain, 1,100 feet at the highest point), past Lake Marie Louise, and past the provincial park to a cove of summer homes on Lake Superior overlooking Silver Islet. (There is a famous silver mine on the tiny island. $3 ¼ million worth taken out by 1884, the year it closed.) I walked a half-hour along the shoreline past modest summer homes...Everybody seemed very friendly as I walked along...The lake was only slightly fretted by the wind, a very mild breeze reaching me. The slightest wisp of cloud on the horizon. The lake is a pristine gentian blue. Very comfortable walking weather...How I'd hate to be stuck out here in one of these isolated summer homes all summer! Here is proof again that one person's heaven is another person's hell.

6:55 p.m. Arrive back from Sibley Provincial Park. Perfectly still and cerulean at the University. Students in cut-offs play frisbee. A few are sprawled on the grass, getting a tan. Today, northern Ontario is heaven!...

Pope Paul the 6th dies today.

TV coverage of Commonwealth Games continues. Canada leads in medal output, especially gold (7), followed by England and New Zealand...

August 7, Monday...The radio ad which seems to ring in my ears most often on local CBQ is: "Colt 45 beer, right here! Colt 45 beer, right here!..."

1:30-2:30 p.m. Visit Kababeka Falls, near a village by the same name (population of 325, according to the Ontario provincial map). The park pamphlet does not state the height of

197

G. Louis Heath, Ph.D.

the falls, but it looks 80 feet or so, straight drop, to me...I walked 40 minutes around the many campsites nestled in the trees on the slope adjacent to the falls opposite the highway (Highway 17/11). Relaxed in a grove of peaceful poplars, the breeze soughing through, cooling me, as a respite from the heat outside the comfort of the shade. Much hotter here, inland a few miles, than anywhere near Lake Superior. I intended to walk a full hour, but cut it short due to the excruciating heat. Will complete the final 20 minutes of my walk in the evening in Thunder Bay...Many vacant campsites, and although quite a few people here, the park is far from full. Only a single row of cars in the huge parking lot...Campground is complete with showers and laundromat...

The voyageurs, in the "Montreal boats," basically huge canoes, laden with trade goods one way, furs the other, portaged these falls on the Kam River, carrying on their backs loads up to 180 pounds each...Quite a few foundered and died under their loads. Few voyageurs were able to work beyond age 40, and, in fact, a high percentage were dead well before attaining that ripe old age...

August 8, Tuesday...11 a.m. Ian Thomas, budding rock star interviewed on "Morningside." Then Don Harron -- a Canadian who is on the "Hee Haw" show as the character "Charlie Farquharson," a character he created -- interviews Annapolis Valley, Nova Scotia writer Ernest Buckler, in Halifax. Harron read from Buckler's **Window On The Sea**, from a selection entitled, "Man and Snow Man." And Buckler himself read a few of his hilarious, iconoclastic poems which appear in his recent book **Whirligig**...I have read two Buckler novels, **The Mountain And The Valley** and **Ox Bells And Fireflies**. They are well-written but not especially to my taste. What I do groove on, however, is his poetry. I keep reading and re-reading it. I have virtually worn out my copy of **Whirligig**, a McClelland and Stewart hardcover that includes mostly poetry, and several of his highly off-the-wall short stories. Wild, wild short stories!...

198

3:30 p.m. Visit the Thunder Bay Historical Museum on May Street...I am especially impressed with a large plaque in memory of the 13 ships and 225 men who were lost in a "terrific storm" on Lakes Superior, Huron, and Erie, November 9th and 10th, 1913...

...Lakehead University Centre is a three-story, huge, rambling building that is faced with orangish-hued blocks of concrete that are a dazzling sight of beauty in the waning golden glow of the setting sun...

6 p.m. Dinner at the Finnish restaurant, Hoito. I have **kalakeitto** (fish stew, $1.45) and **villi** (clabbered milk). The Hoito, a nice clean place with excellent service and a family atmosphere, also offers **voileivat** (open-face sandwiches) and **makkara** sandwiches -- **makkara** means "baloney" in Finnish -- among many other menu items.

August 9, Wednesday...12:30-2 p.m. Lunch with Jeff Retcio, business teacher at "The Soo." Thirty-nine years old, graying, married at age 30, father of a two-year-old son...He told me of a one-week course he took in Toronto where he visited the packaging room of Eaton's. The manager told him he knew women were returning Easter bonnets right after Easter Sunday, but Eaton's preferred to allow them to do it, building up goodwill, in order to eventually sell them bigger items such as refrigerators...Retcio is a Ukrainian. He told me about his Ukrainian friend and neighbor who was a supervisor at the Algoma Steel Plant. He refused to go out on strike and scabbed by doing his men's work when they were on the picket lines. After the strike, when the normal work routine resumed, his men impeded the production process and harassed him so much that he became totally ineffective as a supervisor and management had to transfer him to a new plant, where his reputation followed him, and he was similarly ineffective...

Jeff told me wryly about how he was lying on his bed yesterday, reading about professional negotiations in education, a requirement of the course he's taking, and in the room above

199

him a beautiful Brazilian young lady was tripping about in her stiletto-heeled pumps. "I spent more time fantasizing about her," he grinned, "than reading my assignment, I was so distracted."

Jeff also told me about the fellow who didn't get the chairman job he now holds. He and his wife split up after he didn't get the chairman's job, and when he moved back into the house, she moved out. Over the next few months, he drank himself to death, and was found as a stinking heap of decaying flesh by a neighbor who got a whiff...

Retcio will begin to make arrangements to have a cabin built on a plot of land he owns on the Lake Superior shoreline when he returns to "The Soo" tomorrow. He's anxious to get back to his fine wife and son. "I can count on my wife waiting for me with a great meal," he said. "That's the way she is. I **know** she will want to do that, knowing that I've been eating residence-hall cafeteria food for weeks. She's a great wife."

2:15 p.m. For $1.05, plus 4 cents tax, I buy a 600 gram box of **Tide** laundry soap ("**Tide's** in...Dirt's out." "**Tide** est là...La saleté s'en va.") and go to the laundry room in the residence hall to wash my clothes in preparation for the trip back to Illinois...Read from Hugh Garner's Depression-era novel **Cabbagetown** while my clothes wash. **Cabbagetown** is a great book. It was Canada's first urban novel. I am reading it for the third time...Hugh Garner is my hero. I especially recommend his short stories. **The Hugh Garner Omnibus**, published by McGraw-Hill Ryerson earlier in 1978, contains his best stories, the best of which, to my mind, are "A Trip For Mrs. Taylor" and "Twelve Miles Of Asphalt."

August 11, Friday...1:30 p.m. Close my summer account at the Canadian Imperial Bank of Commerce in the basement of the University Centre. I felt good opening it, as they gave me a plus 10% on my deposit. But , in closing it, they subtracted 14%, reflecting the volatile fluctuation in the value of the Canadian dollar vis-à-vis the U.S. buck the past couple months. I withdrew $1,690. I spent $2,250 on my summer in Thunder Bay...

8:22 p.m. Late dinner at Voyageur Restaurant. While I'm dining, a dozen Boy Scouts from Tennessee pull up in a pair of station wagons, two canoes strapped atop each vehicle. Soon, another unrelated group from Texas, clad in blaze-orange and electric-lime jackets and black leather caps, pull up on Harley-Davidson candy-apple-red motorcycles. The scuzzy woman of this pack, her jacket bears an American flag stylized in the form of a #1. The seven of them don't remove their caps in the restaurant, and their menacing presence envelopes the entire dining room....

Canada has 44 gold medals, 27 silver, on the next to the last day of the Eleventh Commonwealth Games...

I fill up "Old Illinois" with regular at 93.9 cents per Canadian gallon at John C. Maki Shell Station. Her plates this year read, "MY 8396."

August 13, Sunday. Depart-for-Illinois Day. Up at 7 a.m. Three hours to finish packing car and check out of the residence hall. A parking patrolman ("C. McDougall") insists on giving me a $5 ticket for parking near the hall as I pack, even though he can see I'm leaving and it's Sunday and the position of my car is no problem to anyone!...

It begins to rain at 9:35 a.m. and I have to get my umbrella out of the car in order to pack the last few items...I finally get underway, bound south for Duluth on Highway 17/11, which becomes U.S. Highway 61 once into Minnesota...I lose an hour waiting in line, and going through customs, at the "U.S. Border Inspection Station, Grand Portage, Minn./ Clearance 14 Ft. – Trucks Park Right./ Welcome to the United States./ Bienvenue aux États-Unis."

201

About The Author

G. Louis Heath, Ph.D. is the author of the 1973 best-selling book *The New Teacher* published by Harper and Row. He has published several other books, including *The Hot Campus*, *Vandals In The Bomb Factory*, and *Mutiny Does Not Happen Lightly*.

In recent years Dr. Heath has devoted himself to writing short stories, poems, and memoirs, one book of which is *Leaves of Maple*.

Dr. Heath is retired from Illinois State University. He is currently the Chair, Social Science Division, Mount St. Clare College in Clinton, Iowa. He holds B.A., M.A. and Ph.D. degrees from the University of California at Berkeley.

Printed in the United States
998100004B

Sierra Club Bulletin

1925   Ascent of Mt. Merit
1927   Mountaineering in the Rockies
1927   The First Ascent of Mount Russell
February 1928   Climbing the Sierra Nevada from Owens Valley
February 1928   The Sierra Club Ascent of Mount Geike
February 1928   The First Ascent of Mt. Humphreys from the East
April 1938   Skiing and Climbing in the Headwaters
of Bishop Creek

Southern Sierran

February 1961   High Sierra Avalanches
July-August 1961   Thunderstorms in the Sierra Nevada

The Bancroft Library Collection

(Norman Clyde Papers BANC MSS 79/33c, The Bancroft Library, University of California, Berkeley, previously unpublished)

Three Superlatives in the Sequoia
From the Tallest Trees to the Highest Mountain
An Evening Climb of Mt. Muir
Temple Crag in November
Over the Hermit
A Stormy Ascent of Mt. Humphreys
Highest of the Minarets
Over Unicorn and Cathedral Peaks:
the Yosemite National Park
Co-operation in Camping
Comfortable Bivouacking
Cautions for the California Mountaineer

The Clyde manuscripts from the collection of The Bancroft Library were reprinted with special permission. Thomas H. Jukes tribute to Norman Clyde, which first appeared in the American Alpine Club Journal of 1973, was reprinted here with the permission of Mr. Thomas Jukes. Journal entries were transcribed from Norman Clyde's personal journals, while he was still alive, by one of Clyde's climbing partners in the 1950's and 60's, Mrs. Pat Adler-Ingram. "A Tragedy in the Sierra Nevada" is from the collection of the editor.

© 1995 Spotted Dog Press

OTHER BOOKS BY SPOTTED DOG PRESS

CLIMBING MT. WHITNEY
BY WALT WHEELOCK AND WYNNE BENTI

*The original classic with up-to-date permit,
route information, and local history.
Full of photographs. With maps.
Illustration of the East Face by Himalayan
climber Dee Molenaar.
Photographs by Norman Clyde.*

GRAND CANYON TREKS
BY HARVEY BUTCHART

*When he first arrived in Arizona,
who would have thought that the mathematics
professor from America's heartland would some day
be called the "undisputed king of obsessive
Grand Canyon hiking" by Backpacker Magazine.
Butchart was the first to walk over 12,000 miles
through the Canyon in 1,000 days of hiking,
from Lee's Ferry to Lake Mead,
a distance comparable
to hiking halfway around the earth.
Photographs and maps.*

AVAILABLE FROM YOUR LOCAL BOOKSTORE.